FREE Stuff & Good Deals for Folks over 50

by Linda Bowman

FREE Stuff & Good Deals for Folks over 50

by Linda Bowman

SANTA MONICA PRESS

Published by:
SANTA MONICA PRESS LLC
P.O. Box 1076
Santa Monica, CA 90406-1076
1-800-784-9553
www.santamonicapress.com

Printed in the United States

Santa Monica Press books are available at special quantity discounts when
purchased in bulk by corporations, organizations, or groups. Please call
our Special Sales department at 1-800-784-9553.

*This book is intended to provide general information. The publisher, author,
distributor, and copyright owner are not engaged in rendering health, medical,
legal, financial, or other professional advice or services. Be aware that offers,
phone numbers, addresses, web sites, etc. may have changed. The publisher,
author, distributor, and copyright owner are not liable or responsible to any
person or group with respect to any loss, illness, or injury caused or alleged
to be caused by the information found in this book.*

ISBN 1-891661-15-9

Library of Congress Cataloging-in-Publication Data

Bowman, Linda, 1947-
     Free stuff & good deals for folks over 50 / by Linda Bowman
     p. cm.
     ISBN 1-891661-15-9 (pbk.)
     1. Discounts for the aged—United States. 2. Aged—Services
for—United States.   3.Aged—Recreation—United States. 4. Aged—
Travel—United States. I. Title.
     HQ1064.U5 B685 2001
     362.6'0973—dc21

                         00-069693

Book and cover design by Lynda "Cool Dog" Jakovich
Illustrations by Jorge Pacheco

Contents

Have the Time of Your Life in the Prime of Your Life

This book is for those of us who know we are on the threshold of what should and can be the very best years of our lives. There are nearly 70 million Americans over the age of 50. We are as varied, active, interesting, vital and exciting as any group can be. However, as a group, there are only two things we have in common:
1. We were born more than 50 years ago; and
2. We have earned admittance into the incredible, wonderful, wide world of "freebies" and special discounts for folks over 50.

Because of the variety of our interests, abilities, and activities, and the differences between segments within the 50+ age group, there is no name or label that properly identifies everyone. The new definition of "middle age" has been set between the years of 44 and 66. With that being the case, forget the idea of "senior." Most of us between these ages are enjoying the "prime of our life," i.e. Middle Age. For the sake of simplifying terms, I will use "mature adult" and "senior citizen" interchangeably throughout this book, hopefully satisfying the majority of my readers, whether you have just turned 50 or are nearing 90. Since more mature adults claim to feel, on the average, 15 years younger than their chronological age, labels have become nearly meaningless.

Along with the problems of labeling folks 50 and over, are the false assumptions and stereotypes that sometimes accompany those labels:
- Mature adults are all the same;
- Mature adults are always becoming ill and suffer from poor health;
- Mature adults have nothing to contribute to society;
- Mature adults are set in their ways, stubborn, and difficult;
- Mature adults are draining our country of its funds;
- Mature adults are weak and non-influential;
- Mature adults should be retired at age 65;
- Mature adults are poorer than other segments of the population;
- Mature adults are basically lonely;
- Mature adults lose their mental faculties and can't think or reason as well as they used to;
- Mature adults prefer the company of older people like themselves;
- Mature adults are physically inactive and become more sedentary as they get older.

I could go on, but be aware that all of the above statements and any others you've heard are entirely false, foolish and without substance. In fact, in every case the reverse is true:

- You can be healthier, happier, and live longer now than ever before;
- Your financial situation can be significantly better and continue to improve after you reach 50;
- Your relationships and friendships can be deeper and more meaningful than before. Romance can even get better with experience, time, and maturity on your side;
- Your health can remain excellent and you can participate in nearly any physical activity you choose;
- Your mental faculties can be sharper, your senses keener, and your beliefs and needs more focused than they were in your youth;
- Your choices are greater than ever, with more time on your hands and the freedom to do what you want whenever you want;
- You can achieve goals you've always aspired to, rising to new levels of knowledge and ability. Learning and becoming are processes that live as long as you do;
- You can make an important difference in the quality of your life and the lives of all mature adults;
- You alone have the ability and wisdom to cross generational barriers and communicate, teach, and reach out to others of all ages.

Mature adults are the fastest growing segment of the population, representing nearly a quarter of the people in the United States today. As a result, the business community is intensely aware of the purchasing power held by mature adults. With over $1 billion in combined annual income and $300 million in discretionary income, seniors as consumers are a formidable force. In addition, the dozens of senior organizations, associations and advocacy groups representing millions of people over the age of 50 are no longer ignored by our leaders and lawmakers on Capitol Hill. Meeting the growing needs and demands of this group will continue to be a significant challenge in the future.

Products and services that focus on the mature market with freebies, discounts and privileges continue to grow yearly as the number of seniors continues to increase. Some of the areas offering freebies, discounts and great deals that I discuss in this book include:

- Transportation: airlines, car rentals, trains, buses;
- Entertainment: concerts, movies, theater, attractions, theme parks, restaurants, sports events, fairs, museums, zoos, aquariums, historical sites;
- Sports: Senior Olympic and multi-sport competitions, tennis, golf, swimming, walking, skiing, cross-country skiing, dancing, running, biking, bowling;
- Shopping: chain department stores, bookstores, toy stores, home repair services, automobile repair services, medical and dental services, gasoline service stations;
- Travel: cruises, tours, travel clubs, hotels, motels, resorts, free travel, adventure travel, package

deals, national parks and recreation areas, travel with grandchildren;

- Financial Investments, Savings and Insurance: bank and S&L discounts and perks, retirement and investment advice, free insurance information, tax advice;
- Education: travel/study programs, free and low-cost adult education programs, college and university programs, computer networking for seniors;
- Health: health screenings, free information, treatment, preventative programs, medicine and prescription drugs.

These topics include some of the major areas of interest to mature adults. In addition I've included some helpful suggestions and guidelines to aid you in getting these deals and enjoying them as much as possible.

There are some terrific opportunities out there waiting for mature adults. Feeebies and savings can be found nearly everywhere. Not only can you save when you're having fun (which is where most people think all the savings are), but you can save at the bank, where you shop, going back to school, and in your health care needs. You can save from $1 to thousands of dollars, from 10% to 90% by being aware and informed of the hundreds of special senior privileges, discounts and perks available just because you've turned 50. Some of the freebies and deals that I've included are available to all age groups—not just seniors. I just want to make sure you are aware of them.

Ask and You Shall Receive

To take advantage of these deals, all you need to do is ask for them. The two most important questions to ask are:

- "Do you have discounts for seniors?"
- "What is the lowest available rate?"

Memorize these questions and use them everywhere you go to purchase products and services: at restaurants, movies, booking travel arrangements, theater events, sporting events, at the cleaners, at your bank . . . anywhere and everywhere. Soon you will be realizing savings you never thought possible. And they weren't, before this. You have entered a new life and a new world. They say life is a series of passages. Today, being 50 and older means passing through the wide doors of enjoying the best things in life. So why not enjoy them for less and even for free?

Serious Shopping and Savings

Mature adults area loyal group when it comes to shopping and choosing products and services. Smart retailers and companies in the business of serving the public know that mature people want quality and service they can depend on, and will reward those who satisfy their needs by coming back again and again.

Sears has a discount program specifically targeted to seniors. Sears' program, Mature Outlook, offers, among other benefits, significant discounts in the form of coupons that can be used for a variety of products and services.

Other major chain stores that offer senior citizen discounts include:

- Ames Department Stores. Over 455 locations in New England. Offers 10 percent senior citizen discount on unadvertised merchandise. Individual stores have "Senior Discount Day."
- Family Dollar Stores. More than 1,600 stores in 27 states and Washington, D.C. Offers 10 percent senior citizen Tuesday discount on all merchandise.
- Waldenbooks www.borders.com. More than 1,000 stores throughout the country. The "Preferred Reader Program" entitles members to 10 percent discount on all books and accessories (including items on sale). There is a one-time $5 membership fee for those 60 years or older.

Senior citizen newspapers often carry advertising by local establishments for discounts of at least 10 percent. Some discounts are good only on certain days of the week or are offered on a "limited time only" basis. In most cases you need to ask for the discount at the time of purchase or service. Here are some recent examples of discounts:

- 10 percent off toys, games, and hobbies at regional chain of toy stores.
- 15 percent on any purchase, regular or sale, for one day at a popular chain department store.
- Senior citizen discount coupons available from a local taxi company.

- Senior citizen discounts from a distributor of medical, burglary, and fire alarms and security systems.
- 10 percent senior citizen discount for all automotive service repairs from a tire and brake service garage.
- 10 percent discount to seniors over 50 on all orders from a collectibles mail order catalog.
- Senior citizen coupon worth $1 off the cost of a car wash.
- 10 percent senior citizen discount on television repair service.
- 10 percent senior citizen discount on window washing.
- 10 percent senior citizen discount on veterinarian services.
- 20 percent senior citizen discount on medical services of a general practitioner.
- 15 to 25 percent senior citizen discount on dental services.
- 15 percent senior citizen discount on the services of an electrician and 10 percent off the cost of services of a handyman.
- Senior discount offered on house painting, carpentry, and concrete and block work.
- 41 percent senior citizen discount on regular price acrylic yarn from super yarn mart.

If you want to take advantage of self-service prices at gas stations, but have a problem doing it yourself (pumping gas can be hard on stiff joints and limbs), individual station owners are often sympathetic to the less agile older citizen's plight. Speak with the manager or owner about arranging a time to come in for gas when business is usually slow. They will help you fill up at the self-service tank when they are not busy with other customers. Avoid gas station-convenience store combos or high-volume gas stations. Some operate with only one or two cashiers who are unable to leave their posts to help customers.

State senior citizen discount programs include businesses offering senior discounts (in addition to the discounts seniors receive at state parks, campgrounds, fishing areas, historic sites, etc.). A member of the program can use his or her membership card to obtain discounts at establishments participating in the senior discount program. In California, participants advertising in the Yellow Pages of the phone directory display a special symbol in their ads to notify consumers that they belong to the program. Check with your state's Office/Department on Aging for a list of businesses in the senior citizen discount program.

Remember the Internet!

Just a few years ago, the Internet was something only "techies" understood. It was a strange world located in the foreign galaxy of cyberspace that was off limits to all but the most computer-saavy folks. What a difference a few years can make!

Today, I *highly* recommend you learn to use the "net" and "surf" your way to the knowledge and savings that are just a mouse click away. Nearly every commercial and consumer entity now has a web site, and navigation around cyberspace is becoming easier all the time.

If you don't have your own computer, you can use one for free at your local library. If the idea of the Internet is confusing and overwhelming to you, check with your local high school, senior center or adult learning center for free or low-cost courses in using this amazing technological tool. Or, better yet, ask one of your family members or colleagues at work if they would be willing to give you some lessons. Most people, especially adult children and grandchildren are happy to teach you their online skills. This is a great opportunity to bond with a co-worker or younger family member who, in turn, will get the satisfaction of teaching you something that can enhance your life. You can also jump right in, dial up the Internet, and go to "A Seniors' Guide to Going Online" www.qui.com/-shepherd/online.htm. Once you've learned the basics, you will quickly catch on to the shortcuts and tricks of finding nearly everything and anything you desire.

I have included many web sites, in addition to phone numbers and addresses, to make your search for savings and freebies as easy as possible. I encourage you to explore these sites, which, in many cases, will lead you to additional sites and links to help you find exactly what you need.

Welcome to the world of senior savings and have the time of your life in the prime of your life!!

CHAPTER 1

Let Us Entertain You (for Less!)

One of the most exciting and diverse areas for great senior deals and discounts is the area of entertainment. Wherever you go to have a good time and enjoy yourself, you can probably do it for less than the price listed, and sometimes even for free. Some of these attractions and entertainment opportunities include: Movies, dances, company tours, concerts, theme parks, museums, historical sites, theaters, restaurants, tourist attractions, and sporting events.

Always ask about a senior citizen discount before buying a ticket or paying an entrance fee. It's not always advertised that such discounts are available. You should always carry your driver's license (or other proof of age I.D.) or membership card in an over-50 club as proof that you deserve a break. A lot of folks who have kept fit and healthy simply don't look 50 or 55 and may be asked for proof of age. Remember when they used to "card" you when you needed to be 21 to get into a club or other "adult" venue? Here you are again, being asked, "Are you sure you're 50? You don't look it."

Movies and Concerts

Free movies and concerts are some of the most enjoyable events offered nearly everywhere, often on a weekly or monthly basis at the same location. Senior centers, libraries, museums, and public auditoriums make use of their empty spaces and community rooms during the day by running classic movies, educational movies, or special movie series.

There are also free daytime concerts given by musical groups who volunteer their talents in the community. For example, summer concert series and holiday musical performances in shopping centers and malls. Parks and recreation departments also sponsor free events (often aimed at retirees and those who are free from daily jobs and family obligations) such as dances and concerts given by local school bands, dance and music departments.

Many of the performers themselves are retired professionals or working professionals who still perform regularly at "paying" events. These concerts give those who can't afford the steep price of tickets a chance to experience quality musical events.

For example, the following free events were recently listed in my local metropolitan newspaper:

- George Coleman and the Harold Mabern Quartet kick off the "Summer Nights At MOCA" weekly summer series featuring jazz and blues performances, wine and beer tastings and gallery tours at the Museum of Contemporary Art. 5–8 P.M.
- The Playboy Jazz Festival presents "Jazz on Film," a two-hour compilation of film clips

featuring classic performances by Charlie Parker, Dexter Gordon, Billie Holiday, Chet Baker, Dinah Washington, Willie "The Lion" Smith and others, at the Los Angeles County Museum of Art. 7:30 P.M. Admission is free.

• Trumpeter Jeff Beal's combo performs with pianist Alan Pasqua at the Los Angeles County Museum of Art, 5:50–8:30 P.M.

• "Music Under the Stars" features the Pasadena Pops Orchestra and the Gospel Choirs of First AME Church of Los Angeles performing music by Leonard Bernstein, Tchalkovsky and others, outdoors at Pasadena City Hall, 7:30 P.M.

• Laura Krafft hosts the comedy variety show "The Extravaganza at ImprovOlympic West," 9 P.M.

Additionally, you can nearly always save money off the adult ticket price at first-run movies. Discounts run from 25–75% off regular ticket prices. With the price of movie tickets at $8.00 and rising, this is an important discount if you enjoy going to the movies.

Fairs and Expos

Festivals, expos, state and country fairs, circuses, and special interest shows also offer substantial discounts for seniors. Auto shows, house and garden shows, antique shows, holiday fairs, ski shows, recreational vehicle shows, boat shows, travel shows, arts and crafts shows, gift shows, and even air shows often have senior discounts on admission prices.

Eat for Cheap (or Free)

Over the past several years, the restaurant industry has found it pays to be good to their older patrons, who are among the largest percentage of repeat customers.

A simple way to eat for cheap, in fact for free, is to patronize restaurants that have special "Happy Hours." These are held during the slow hours (usually between 4 and 6 P.M.) when restaurants are looking for business before the normal dinner rush. These establishments offer specially priced drinks and free hors d'oeurves that would easily make a tasty, filling meal. If you live in a large city, chances are that many of the different ethnic restaurants offer a "Happy Hour" to entice new customers to try their special type of cuisine. In fact, one restaurant in Venice, California advertises a "Sushi Happy Hour" during the week.

Restaurants with popular bars often feature a delicious array of free food that changes nightly. Although you have to order a drink, it needn't be an alcoholic one. Juices and soft drinks will do quite well. And the delicious rewards on the hors d'oeurves table are well worth the price of a drink. (By the way, if you are a football fan, don't forget "Monday Night Football." Look for bars and restaurants with large screen televisions that advertise "FREE" food for coming in to watch the game and have a drink.)

"Early Bird Dinners" and "Sunset Meals" are especially popular with budget-minded diners who value quality food at good prices. Generally, a main course, vegetable, dessert, and beverage are included at a price lower that what the main course alone would cost during regular hours. Although they apply to everyone, these meals are targeted to seniors who often prefer to eat their evening meal early (sometimes making it their main meal of the day). Most restaurants offer "Early Bird dinners" until 6:30 or 7:00 P.M.

Many individual restaurants offer senior citizen discounts on regular menu items or have a special senior menu with lower prices. Some feature two-for-one dinners (for seniors or anyone). You can usually find these specials in the restaurant section of your neighborhood newspaper or senior publication. If you are not sure whether a restaurant has a senior special, ask for it.

Several national and regional restaurant chains offer senior citizen discounts. A few, like Denny's, are especially interested in the preferences and concerns of their older patrons. And for good reason. Adults over 55 make up nearly one-third of all Denny's customers patronizing their 1,500 restaurants. Depending on the individual restaurant chain's policy, discounts may be identical everywhere or may differ slightly from location to location. The restaurant may issue "membership" cards valid at all locations to seniors who patronize them frequently. Here are some examples of senior discounts at restaurant chains:

1 Potato 2 www.1potato2.com offers a 10 percent discount on any purchase for those over 62. Ninety-nine outlets throughout United States and Japan.

Arby's www.arby.com offers a 10 to 20 percent food discount, a free beverage with your meal and free coffee. Age requirements may vary from 55 to 60+ depending on management's program. Not every location offers the discount program.

Denny's has a Senior Menu, which includes smaller portions for breakfast, lunch and dinner items. There is also a nightly dinner special that changes every day.

Holiday Inn restaurants give Mature Outlook members 10 percent off their food bill. Those belonging to the Holiday Inn Travel Venture Club also receive food discounts.

Red Lion Inns www.redlion.com and Thunderbird Motor Inns www.thunderbirdmotorinn.com will give card-carrying members of AARP, Mature Outlook, and Silver Saver's Passport a 15 percent discount on regularly priced food items. 800-233-0827.

Residence Inn by Marriott. AARP members receive 10 percent off room rates according to availability. Breakfast is complimentary with room stay.

Burger King. Buy any food item at regular the price and get a beverage for twenty-five cents.

Pizza Hut offers 10 percent off the full meal price for seniors 65+. Varies from location to location.

Bob's Big Boy family restaurants offer 10 percent off any meal, at anytime for anyone in a party that includes one person over 55. Bob's Big Boy Senior's Discount Cards are valid at all locations.

Sizzler restaurants Senior Club members (55 and older) are entitled to 20 percent off any regular menu item every day from 2 to 5 P.M. and all day Monday, Tuesday and Wednesday. They also have a Senior Menu with light and lean items.

International House of Pancakes www.ihop.com offers seniors a "limited time only" coupon offer of a complete special dinner after 4 P.M.

Mr. Steak has a Senior Dinner program that gives a 10 percent discount (before taxes) on regularly priced meals at restaurants displaying a "Senior Diner" symbol.

Tastee Freez International www.tastee-freez.com has determined that older folks are their number one consumers of dipped ice cream and gives a 10 percent discount to its "Gold Club" members at participating locations around the country.

TCBY www.tcby.com frozen yogurt stores offer seniors the "Golden Discount Program" giving them 10 percent off the price of a single menu item and 20 percent off items through promotional mailing programs.

Dutch Pantry restaurants (located in PA, DL, NC, OH and WV) give senior citizen discounts of 10 percent off all regular menu items.

Here are some examples of senior discounts at restaurants in the New York area:

Antonio Ristorrante. 140 W. 13th St. 212-645-4606. 10 percent Senior Discount.

Kameda Japanese Restaurant. 71 University Place (between 10th and 11th Streets). 212-673-0634. 20 percent off prices every day from 5:30–7 P.M. on purchases of $14 or more.

Lucien. 14 First Avenue (at 1st Street). 212-260-6481. 20 percent off prices every day from 5-7 P.M.

St. Dymphna Restaurant. Handicap facilities. 118 St. Mark's Place. 212-254-6636. 20 percent off every day.

Tiffin Indian Vegetarian. 18 Murray Street (between Broadway and Church). 212-533-9306. 10 percent off every day.

China Fun. 246 Columbus Avenue (at 72nd St). 212-752-0810. 30 percent off for 60+ seniors.

Mendy's West. 208 W. 70th St. (between Amsterdam & West End Avenues). 212-877-6787. 15 percent off prices of Kosher entree Mondays through Thursdays from 4–6 P.M. along with "All You Can Eat" salad bar.

Polanco. 502 Amsterdam Avenue (between 84th and 85th Streets). 212-799-1434. 10 percent discount Mondays through Thursdays from 4–10:30 P.M.

La Stanza Verde. 338 W. 46th St. 212-974-8897. 10 percent off Tuesdays through Saturdays from 4:30 to 11:30 P.M.

Bernie's Place. 1217 Avenue J. 718-677-1515. 10 percent off Mondays through Thursdays from 4–6:30 P.M. for Kosher vegetarian and dairy food.

China Buffet. 1552 Ralph Avenue. 718-241-1624. 10 percent off the $8.95 "All You Can Eat" buffet every day from 4–11 P.M.

Deli 52. 5120 Thirteenth Avenue. 718-436-4830. Five percent off Monday through Saturday from 12:30–5:30 P.M.

Del Prado Coffee Shop. 88 Fifth Avenue. 718-399-2630. 10 percent off every day, all day.

Demu Café. 773 Fulton St. 718-875-8484. 10 percent off every day.

Fuji Hanna. 512 Avenue U. 718-336-3888. Five percent off Kosher dinner menus Monday through Thursdays from 4:30–6:30 P.M.

Savings at Unusual Restaurants

Some combination dinner/theater attractions also give seniors a break. These include:

Arabian Nights Dinner Attraction www.arabian-nights.com in Kissimmee, Florida. 800-553-6116. $6 off regular $36.95 admission price for seniors (over 55). For further information contact Silvia Baum, Reservations Manager. Email: Reservations@Arabian-Nights.com.

Hornblower Dining Yachts. 800-ON-THE-BAY. Operate in California harbors. 10 percent senior citizen discounts on all regularly scheduled dining cruises.

Medieval Times. 800-229-8300. Kissimmee, Florida and Buena Park, California. 10 percent off for senior citizens, and an additional 10 percent if you are an AAA member.

M.S. Dixie dinner cruises www.tahoedixie2.com. Lake Tahoe, California. 775-588-3508. Seniors (60 and over) receive a $2 per person discount on any M.S. Dixie II cruise and a $4 per person discount on their 5 P.M. Emerald Bay Sightseeing/Dinner Cruise with dinner (available mid-June to end of August only). Ask for your discount at the ticket booth when purchasing tickets. Any questions, email Bill Chernock: bcts1@sierra.net. Mailing Address: P.O. Box 1667, Zephyr Cove, NV 89448. Physical Address: 760 Highway 50, Zephyr Cove, NV 89448.

Tourist Attractions

Most tourist attractions around the country give special rates to senior visitors. Members of local or regional senior citizen organizations and clubs may also be entitled to special savings off entrance fees. Many attractions advertise special "limited time only" discounts for seniors at certain times of the year. These special promotions are often lower than the regular senior discounts. Some well known U.S. attractions that offer senior citizen discounts include:

Boot Hill Museum www.boothill.org. Dodge City, Kansas. 316-227-8188. From Boot Hill: "Our senior discount is fifty cents off the regular adult ticket price. Off-season senior admission is $5.50. From May 27 through August senior admission is $6.50. Your admission ticket gives you access to view all of the exhibits and buildings in the Boot Hill Museum complex. Additional tickets must be purchased in the Boot Hill Museum Gift shop and the General Rath Store." Further information email: frontst@pld.com.

Coral Reef State Park. Key Largo, Florida. 305-451-1202.

The Empire State Building www.esbnyc.com. New York, New York. 212-736-3100. Senior Discount is $7.

The Florida Golf Guide Area Attractions. 407-363-8000.

Gatorland. Orlando, Florida. 407-855-5496 or 1-800-393-JAWS.

Grand Canyon Caverns, between Kingman and Seligman, Arizona. 502-422-3223/3224. Senior Discount is $8.50.

Meteor Crater. Flagstaff, Arizona. 800-842-7293.

New Orleans Steamboat Company www.nosteam boat.com. New Orleans, Louisiana. 800-233-BOAT.

Palm Springs Aerial Tramway www.pstramway.com. Palm Springs, California. 888-515-TRAM. Senior Discount is $17.65, 55yrs+.

Queen Mary and Spruce Goose www.sprucegoose.org. Long Beach, California. 213-499-1629.

Santa's Workshop, North Pole. Colorado Springs, CO. 719-684-9432.

The United Nations www.un.org. New York, New York. 212-963-4475.

Universal Studios. Orlando, Florida. 407-363-8000. Hollywood, California. 818-777-3762.

All three major television networks invite viewers to see their favorite shows. To receive tickets, send a self-addressed stamped envelope to:

NBC Tickets: 3000 W. Alameda Blvd., Burbank, CA 91523;

CBS Tickets: 7800 Beverly Blvd, Los Angeles, CA 90036;

ABC Tickets: 4151 Prospect Avenue, Hollywood, CA 90027.

For a calendar of television program taping schedules write: Audiences Unlimited, 100 Universal City Plaza, Building 153, Universal City, CA 91608.

Visit a Magic Kingdom for Less

People of all ages are fascinated by amusement and theme parks. For most of us, one visit is never enough. I love going with my children, my grandchildren, my friends and, of course, out of town guests. Most amusement parks offer senior citizen discounts. Of particular note is the Disney Magic Years Club, which entitles those over 60 to year-round reduced prices at both Disneyland and Walt Disney World. It is also good for discounts on parking, meals, shops, some Hilton hotels and National Car Rental locations. Members also receive a quarterly newsletter and vacation packages at Walt Disney World, Disneyland and other locations.

A sampling of other major amusement/theme parks that offer senior discounts include:

Adventure Island www.go2orlando.com. Tampa, Florida. 813-988-5171.

Busch Gardens. Tampa Florida. 813-987-5082. Senior Discount is $37.95 (55 yrs.+).

Cedar Point. Sandusky Ohio. 419-626-0830.

Church Street Station. Orlando, Florida. 407-422-2434. Senior Discount price is $14.95 (Regular Admission: $17.95).

Cypress Gardens. Tampa, Florida. 800-282-2123. Price with senior discount is $27.15.

The Great Escape Fun Park www.sixflags.com/greatescape. Lake George, NY. 518-792-3500.

Hershey Park www.800hershey.com. Hershey, Pennsylvania. 800-1-HERSHEY. Hotel Hershey 800-533-3131. Senior Discount $17.95 for any one over 55. $13.95 over 70 years. Gardens $4.50.Overnight stays are discounted with AARP memberships Email: info@hersheyPA.com for more information.

Knott's Berry Farm www.knotts.com. Buena Park, California. 714-220-5200. Adults: $38. Seniors (60 or over): $28. After 4 P.M. all tickets are $16.95.

Libertyland Amusement Park. Memphis, Tennessee. 901-274-1776. Adults: $20. Seniors 55 and over: Free!

Marineland of Florida www.marineland.hyper mart.net. Marineland, Florida. 904-460-1275.

Marine World Africa USA www.sixflags.com/marineworld. Vallejo, California. 707-643-ORCA. To reach Six Flag's World's Administrative offices call: 707-644-4000. Adult: $34; Senior Discount/Disable (over 60): $25.

Sea World. Orlando, Florida. 800-327-2424 or 407-351-3600. Senior Discount is 10 percent off admission price.

Silver Springs, Florida www.go2orlando.com. 800-234-7458 or 352-236-2121.

Six Flags Over America www.sixflags.com. Eureka, Missouri. 314-938-4800. Senior Discount price is

$17.49. Valencia, California. 818-367-5965 or 661-255-4100. Senior Half Price: $19.50. Atlanta, Georgia. 770-948-9290. Senior Discount Price is $18.50 plus tax.

Universal Studios www.go2orlando.com. Orlando, Florida. 407-363-8000. Senior Discount is fifteen percent off regular price of $39.75.

Waterworld USA. Sacramento, California. Senior Discount (over 60): $5.

Watch and Wager for Less

The races (dog and horse) are another exciting pastime that is popular among mature adults. Race courses around the country offer senior discounts, free "senior" days, "senior matinees" and "half-price" senior discounts. A few tracks offering discounts include the following (check your local race courses for discounts):

Churchill Downs. Louisville, Kentucky. 502-636-4450.

Daytona Beach Kennel Club www.daytonabeachusa.com/recsports.html. Daytona Beach, Florida. 904-252-6484. Seniors are admitted free on matinees.

Earl Warren Showgrounds www.earlwarren.com. Santa Barbara, California. 805-687-0766.

Meadowlands Racetrack www.thebigm.com. East Rutherford, New Jersey. 201-THE-BIG-M; 201-843-2446.

Northeast Florida Kennel Clubs. Jacksonville, Florida. 904-798-9148 or 800-733-2668.

If You're Looking for Culture

From art, science and industry, natural history and sports museums to zoos, botanical gardens, planetariums, and historical landmarks, seniors will find a wide array of educational and cultural attractions that offer senior discounts throughout the year. They are found in every city in the country, rural areas, and out-of-the-way places. Astounding, awesome, and breathtaking, the treasures, beauty and experiences of these places will fill your days with wonderful and lasting memories.

Besides the fact that many government-run institutions and establishments admit seniors for free (including rides, special exhibits, transportation and events inside the attractions) these places offer interesting and stimulating insights into how this country was founded and built. Check with individual organizations for pertinent information including days and hours, senior discounts, "free" days, wheelchair access, current exhibits and special programs, membership information and services, guided tours, etc. Remember, always ask for your discount and present your identification before paying admission.

If you're visiting New York, you should definitely think about purchasing a City Pass. With City Pass, you can visit six famous New York City museums and attractions for one low price. In addition to the American Museum of Natural History, the following attractions are included in the CityPass: Empire State Building Observatory, The Guggenheim Museum, Top of the World Trade Center, Intrepid Sea Air Space Museum, and the Museum of Modern Art. CityPass can be purchased at any museum entrance and is good for 9 days from the date of purchase. Senior Discount: $21.75. Regular Admission: $32.00.

Cultural Attractions

Abby Aldrich Rockefeller Folk Art Museum www.artcom.com/museums. Williamsburg, Virginia. 804-229-1000.

Arlington National Cemetery. Arlington, Virginia. 703-683-2007.

Berkeley Municipal Rose Gardens. Berkeley, California. 510-644-6530.

Betsy Ross House. Philadelphia, Pennsylvania. 215-627-5343.

Birmingham Museum of Art www.artsbma.org. Birmingham, Alabama. 205-254-2566.

California Afro-American Museum. Los Angeles, California. 213-744-7432.

California Museum Of Science and Industry www.usc.edu/dept/ccr/msi.html. Los Angeles, California. 213-744-7400.

California State Capitol Building (tour). Sacramento, California. 916-445-2841.

Chicago Mercantile Exchange www.cme.com. Chicago, Illinois. 312-930-1000.

Davey Crockett Birthplace Park. Limestone, TN. 423-267-2167.

Death Valley National Monument. Death Valley, California. 760-786-2331.

Franklin Mint Museum of Medallic Art. Franklin Center, Pennsylvania. 215-459-6875.

Haleakala National Park, Haleakala, Hawaii. 808-572-4400.

Hawaii Volcanos National Park. Hawaii. 808-985-6000. Golden Age Passports admitted for a one time fee of $10. Golden Eagle Passports admitted free.

Huntington Library. San Marino, California. 818-405-2141.

Independence Hall www.ushistory.org/iha.html. Philadelphia, Pennsylvania. 215-925-7877.

J. Paul Getty Museum. Los Angeles, California. 310-440-7300.

Lincoln Home National Historic Site www. nps.gov/liho. Springfield, Illinois. 217-492-4241, ext. 221 for the Visitor Center.

Lyndon B. Johnson Space Center www.jsc.nasa. gov. Houston, Texas. 281-483-8693.

Montezuma National Wildlife Refuge www.fws. gov/r5mnwr. Seneca Falls, New York. 315-568-5987.

Mount Rushmore National Memorial www.nps. gov/moru. Keystone, South Dakota. 605-574-2523. Golden Age Passports are not accepted.

NASA Visitors Center www.nasa.gov/siteindex. html. Hampton, Virginia. 804 722-2567.

National Hall Of Fame for Famous American Indians www.artcom.com/museums/nv/mr/73055.htm. Anarko, Oklahoma. 405-247-5555. Free Admission.

Naval Aviation Museum www.naval-air.org. Pensacola, Florida. 850-452-3604.

Old Mint Museum. San Francisco, California. 415-774-6830.

Redwood National Park www.nps.gov/redw. Crescent City, California. 707-464-6101.

Scripps Aquarium Museum www.aquarium. ucsd.edu. La Jolla, California. 858-534-FISH. Senior Discount price is $7.50 (over 60).

Temple Square. Norman Temple, The Tabernacle. Salt Lake City, Utah. 801-531-2534.

The Alamo www.thealamo.org. San Antonio, Texas. 210-225-1391.

Tomb of the Unknown Soldier. Arlington, Virginia. 703-683-2007.

Ulysses S. Grant Home. Galena, Illinois. 815-777-0248.

University of California www.mip.berkeley.edu/garden. Botanical gardens, art museum, Worth Ryder Gallery, herbarium, paleontology museum. Berkeley, California. 510-643-2755. Senior Discount: $2 (65 and over).

U.S. Coast Guard Academy www.cga.edu. New London, Connecticut. 860-444-8444.

Valley Forge National Historical Park www.nps.gov/VAFO. Valley Forge, Pennsylvania. 610-783-1077.

West Point Museum www.usma.edu/museum. West Point, New York. 914-938-4041.

Wright Brothers National Memorial www.nps.gov/wrbr. Kitty Hawk, North Carolina. 252-441-7430.

Washington, D.C. for Free

Our nation's capitol, Washington, D.C., has more than three dozen free places of interest, museums, and historical sites, including The Bureau of Engraving and Printing, The F.B.I., Ford's Theater and Lincoln Museum, The Kennedy Center, The Library of Congress, The National Gallery of Art, The Smithsonian Institution Group Museums, The Capitol, The White House, The National Archives, etc. This city is like a giant candy store full of free and exciting sights. For a free booklet that describes major attractions, information on parking, neighborhoods, The Metro, theaters, etc. write: D.C. Convention and Visitors Association, Attn: Tourist Info, 1212 New York Avenue, NW Washington, DC 20005.

You can take a VIP tour of the White House held every Tuesday through Saturday from 10:00 AM to 12 Noon. Contact: White House, 1600 Pennsylvania Avenue, NW, Washington, DC 20500; 202-456-7041. Or to make a reservation, contact your state Senator or Representative at The Capitol, Washington, DC 20515. You can also visit the official White House web site at: www.whitehouse.gov.

There is also a free 100 page directory, "The Gold Mine Directory," that lists more than 2,000 Washington area businesses that provide discounts for people age 60 and over including hotels, inns, restaurants, entertainment facilities, shops, art galleries, bookstores and sightseeing tours. For a copy contact: The D.C. Committee to Promote Washington, 415 12th St., NW, Suite 312, Washington, DC 20004.

Nature

Dallas Zoo. Dallas, Texas. 214-670-5656. $4 Seniors. $6 regular admission.

Indianapolis Zoo www.indyzoo.com. Indianapolis, Indiana. 317-630-2001. Seniors $7. $9.75 regular admission. Parking is $3.

Milwaukee County Zoo www.milwaukeezoo.org. Milwaukee, Wisconsin. 414-771-5500. Seniors $7. $8 regular admission.

Missouri Botanical Garden www.mobot.org. St. Louis, Missouri. 314-577-5100. Seniors $3. $5 regular admission, free admission Wed and Sat.

Monterey Bay Aquarium www.mbayaq.org. Monterey, California. 831-648-4800. Seniors $12.95 (65 and over). Disabled $7.95. Regular admission $15.95.

The National Aquarium www.aqua.org. Baltimore, MD. 410-481-SEAT. Seniors $10.50 Regular admission $14.00.

The Oakland Zoo www.oaklandzoo.org. Oakland, California. 510-632-9525. Seniors $3.50 Regular Admission $6.50.

Philadelphia Zoo www.phillyzoo.org. Philadelphia, Pennsylvania. 215-243-1100. Seniors $8 (over 65). Regular admission $10.50.

John G. Shedd Aquarium www.sheddnet.org. Chicago, Illinois. 312-939-2438. Senior Discount $9 (over 65). Regular Admission $13.

The Steinhart Aquarium www.calacademy.org. Golden Gate Park, San Francisco, California. 415-750-7145. Senior Discount $5.50. Regular Admission $8.50.

Museums

American Craft Museum. New York, New York. 212-956-3535. Senior Discount $2.50. Regular Admission $5.50.

American Museum of Natural History and Hayden Planetarium www.amnh.org. New York, New York. 212-769-5900. Senior Discount $7.50. Regular Admission $10.

Art Institute of Chicago. Chicago, Illinois. 312-889-5100. Suggested donation is $8, free on Tuesdays.

The B & O Railroad Museum. Baltimore, Maryland. 410-752-2490. $15 admission. No Senior Discount.

Denver Art Museum www.denverartmuseum.org. Denver, Colorado. 303640-4433. Senior Discount $2. Regular Admission $4.50.

Fine Arts Museum of San Francisco www. thinker. org/deyoung. San Francisco, California. 415-863-3330. Senior Discount $5 (over 65). Regular Admission $7.

The Frank Lloyd Wright Home and Studio Foundation www.wrightplus.org. Oak Park, Illinois. 708-848-1976. Senior Discount $6 (over 65). Regular Admission $8.

Gene Autry Western Heritage Museum www.autry-museum.org. Los Angeles, California. 213-667-2000. Senior Discount $5. Regular Admission $7.50.

George C. Page Museum www.tarpits.org, Los Angeles, California. 323-936-2230. Senior Discount $3 (over 62). Regular Admission $6.

International Museum of Photography at the George Eastman House www.eastman.org. Rochester, New York. 716-271-3361. Senior Discount $5. Regular Admission $6.50.

The Jewish Museum. New York, New York. 212-423-3318. Senior Discount $5. Regular Admission $8.

Los Angeles County Museum of Art. Los Angeles, California. 323-857-6000. Senior Discount $5 (over 62). Regular Admission $7.

The Metropolitan Museum of Art www.metmuseum.org. New York, New York. 212-535-7710. Suggested senior citizen admission $10.

Monticello www.monticello.org. Charlottesville, Virginia. 804-984-9822. Admission $7. No Senior Discount.

Museum of Contemporary Art. San Diego, California. 858-454-3541. Senior Discount $2. Regular Admission $4.

Museum of Modern Art www.moma.org. New York, New York. 212-708-9400. Senior Discount $6.50 (over 65). Regular Admission $10.

National Air and Space Museum www.nasm.edu. Washington DC. 202-357-2700. Senior Discount $4.50. Regular Admission $5.

National Cowboy Hall of Fame www.cowboyhall offame.org. Oklahoma City, Oklahoma. 405-478-2250. Senior Discount $7. Regular Admission $8.50.

The Paul Revere House www.paulreverehouse. org. Boston, Massachusetts. 617-523-2338. Senior Discount $2.00. Regular Admission $2.50.

The Solomon R. Guggenheim Museum www. guggenheim.org. New York, NY. 212-423-3500. Senior Discount: $7. Regular Admission $12.

University Museum of Archeology and Anthrology www.upenn.edu/museum. Philadelphia, Pennsylvania. 215-898-4001. Senior Donation: $2.50. Regular Donation $5.

Whitney Museum of American Art www.echonyc. com. New York, New York. 212-570-3676. Senior Discount $8. Regular Admission $10.

The performing arts are also popular activities where seniors get a break. From theater, symphony, and ballet to circuses and acrobatic troupes, seniors can enjoy many days and nights of first-class, first-run professional performances at special discounted rates from 25 to 50 percent off regular priced tickets. In the past several years, ticket prices have risen markedly, reaching $70 to $125 for single tickets. Most senior discounts offer significant savings that are sometimes greater at matinees and less popular performances.

There are also "rush" tickets that go on sale the day of a performance that are often 50 percent or more off the face price. A popular theater at the Music Center in Los Angeles offers $10 Public Rush Tickets that are available 10 minutes before curtain time. That's a 75 percent savings off the lowest price $40 ticket! Also, check for preview performance discounts prior to official public openings. This same theater in Los Angeles was offering the best seats in the house for $20 during the preview period. If you can get several people together, you may qualify for senior group rates with reduced prices. Some performing art organizations even offer special "senior performances" and "senior afternoon concerts." Again, it's important to inquire with box office personnel about all the possible savings opportunities before you purchase your tickets.

Sporting Events

Football, baseball, basketball, tennis, track and field, hockey, etc., generally take place in stadiums, auditoriums, and arenas that offer senior discounts for sport events held there during the year. The same stadium may be home to more than one team or host several independent events throughout the year. Check with the office of the teams or the public relations department at the stadium for individual and group senior discounts, year-round discount cards, or special membership opportunities. During regular playing season, there are often one or more senior citizen days. Many teams will even give freebies (pennants, caps, souvenirs) to seniors who ask for them. These are advertised in the local newspaper and in the team's season calendar listing special events and dates. Individual and special multi-day sports events also offer senior citizen discounts.

Also, if you're a real fan, write to your favorite team for a free fan package that generally includes team photos, calendars of games, decals and more. Send a postcard or self-addressed stamped envelope and they will mail you back a goodie package for free. You can look up your team in your phone book, write or call the league headquarters, or call the arena or stadium where they play their home games.

CHAPTER 2

Sports, Fitness and Exercise

As we move through the year 2001, the continuing emphasis on fitness and exercise will affect us all. This is especially true for seniors, as local, state, and national programs continue to thrive with the increase in participation by this age group. Pick up any magazine or newspaper targeted for seniors and you will find numerous opportunities to engage in healthful exercise programs and sports activities. Exercise is not only accepted, but it is strongly encouraged by every major medical association and organization for healthy seniors who want to live longer, fuller lives. In fact, it is nearly impossible to find a sport today that is not being enjoyed by older adults.

Along with the healthful benefits of participating in sports is the added benefit that most sports, exercise, and fitness programs can be enjoyed at substantially reduced prices. In fact, many charges are completely waived simply because you are a senior. Imagine spending a glorious day on the ski slopes for absolutely free, while others have spent up to $70 for a one-day lift ticket!

Calling All Athletes

The US National Senior Sports (formerly known as the U.S. National Senior Olympics) have been held every two years since they began at Washington University in St. Louis in 1987. In order to compete, an athlete must be 55 years or older, and must qualify at a local or state competition sanctioned by the U.S. National Senior Sports Organization (USNSO).

There are more than 500 separate events in archery, badminton, half-court basketball, bicycling, bowling, track and field, golf, horseshoes, race-walking, 5K and 10K road races, shuffleboard, softball, swimming, table tennis, tennis, volleyball, and the triathlon. Competitions are organized for men and women and are separated into age categories. For additional information on qualification requirements and schedules of qualifying games, contact: U.S. National Senior Sports Organization, 83 Princeton Avenue, Hopewell, NJ 08525. 609-466-0022. Web site: www.amgolftour.com.

State Competitions

Several states hold their own senior games, some alternating seasons similar to the summer and winter Olympics. The games often take place at local college or state university campuses. Athletes competing in these games go on to participate in the U.S. National

Senior Sports Classic. In addition to the states listed below, there are programs sponsored by county, city, and local agencies, which participate in the national program. Some state parks and recreation departments are also involved in senior competitions affiliated with the national games.

International Senior Olympics (Information on Senior Games worldwide)—455 North Boulevard, Suite #2001, Baton Rouge, LA 70802. Phone: 504-379-9211; Toll Free 800-331-9211.

California Senior Olympics are held annually in Palm Springs. Contact: California Senior Olympics, 550 North Palm Canyon Drive, Palm Springs, CA 92262. There is also a Northern California Senior Olympics and a San Diego Senior Olympics.

The Pasadena Senior Center offers Olympic programs: 85 E. Holly Street, Pasadena, CA 91103.

Colorado hosts the Rocky Mountain Senior Games twice a year, in summer and winter. Contact: Senior Sports Development Council, Greeley Senior Activity Center, 1010 6th Street, Greeley, CO 80631. 970-350-9433. Web site: www.rmseniorgames.com/about_us.htm.

Connecticut Senior Olympics include physical fitness activities and a health fair. Contact: Connecticut Senior Olympics, Harvey Hubbell Gymnasium, University of Bridgeport, Bridgeport, CT 06601.

Florida's Golden Age Games are held in Sanford annually in November. Contact: Lisa Jones, Sanford Parks & Recreation Dept., PO Box 1788, Sanford, FL 32772. 407-330-5697.

New York Senior Games are held in the spring and are open to state residents up to 80+. Contact: New York Senior Games, State. Parks, Agency 1, 12th Fl., Albany, NY 12238.

North Carolina holds local games throughout the state. Winners compete in the state finals in Raleigh. Contact: North Carolina Senior Games, PO Box 33590, Raleigh, NC 27606.

Pennsylvania Senior Games are a four-day event held at a University campus. Contact: Pennsylvania Senior Games, 231 State St., Harrisburg, PA 17101.

Vermont holds the Green Mountain Senior Games in early fall in Poultney, Vermont. Contact: Green Mountain Senior Games PO Box 1660, Station A, Rutland, VT 05701.

Virginia holds its Golden Olympics in the spring at Lynchburg College. Contact: Golden Olympics, PO Box 2774, Lynchburg, VA 24501.

In Washington, the Seattle Senior Sports Festival is a Regional Qualifying Event for the national games. Contact: Senior Sports Festival, 100 Dexter Ave. North, Seattle, WA 98109-51909

Senior Sports competitions are also held in Alabama, Arizona, Arkansas, Georgia, Idaho, Illinois, Indiana, Iowa, Kansas, Kentucky, Louisiana, Maine, Maryland, Minnesota, Mississippi, Nebraska, Nevada, New Hampshire, New Jersey, New Mexico, Ohio, Oklahoma, Rhode Island, South Carolina, South Dakota, Tennessee, Texas, Washington DC, Wisconsin and Wyoming.

Since 1987 Huntsman Chemicals has sponsored the World Senior Games for senior athletes 50 and above each October in Utah. Senior athletes from all parts of the world are invited to participate in events including golf, swimming, bicycling, tennis, race-walking, track and field, softball, bowling and racquetball. For information contact: Huntsman World Senior Games, 82 West 700 South, St. George, Utah 84770. 800-562-1268. Web site: www.seniorgames.net.

The National Senior Sports Association

The National Senior Sports Association is a non-profit organization that assists active people over 50 in their pursuit of physical and emotional health through active sports participation. The NSSA organizes tournaments (competitive as well as recreational) in tennis, bowling, golf, skiing, and fishing at resorts around the country. They also organize sports-oriented vacations with special group rates. Members receive discounts on a variety of sports equipment and related products, information on national and international sports-related trips, a monthly newsletter, the opportunity to participate in a vacation home exchange program, and names and addresses of members in other locations. For complete information on the NSSA, write them at: NSSA, Suite 204, 301 North Harrison Street, Princeton, NJ 08540. 800-282-6772; 1-800-PLAYS18 (1-800-752-9718).

Tennis—The Sport for a Lifetime

Senior tennis is a thriving and popular sport. There are senior tournaments and competitions held at every level of play. Check with your local parks and recreation department, health or tennis club for information on tournament play for seniors. Also, county tennis associations sponsor tournament play for seniors. If your local park or community center doesn't have any organized program, the United States Tennis Association has compiled a kit that shows how to launch teams of players of the same level of play. You can get the kit by sending $6.50 to: Publications, USTA Center for Education and Recreational Tennis, 70 West Red Oak Lane, White Plains, New York 10604. Ask for the Recreational Senior Tennis League kit.

The USTA holds Senior National Championships each year at tennis facilities throughout the country. There are divisions for men's and women's singles and doubles, from age 30 through 85, Father-Son Doubles and Mother-Daughter Doubles. Write the USTA at 1212 Avenue of the Americas, New York, NY 10036 for their Senior National Championship brochure, which includes dates of play, locations, requirements, and fees. The USTA also publishes a "Senior Tennis Directory." You can write for this guide and a complete list of current USTA Tennis Publications at: USTA,

Publications Department, 70 West Red Oak Lane, White Plains, New York 10604. For additional information check out the USTA web site: www.usta.com.

The USTA/Volvo Tennis League provides a framework for team competition at local levels, culminating in playoffs in which teams travel outside their local area playing a series of championships at district, sectional and national levels. The league offers senior competition in every USTA section of the United States except the Caribbean.

Run for Your Life

The 50-Plus Runners Association www.50plus.org promotes the exchange of information between the growing numbers of over-50 runners. Formed by researchers from Stanford University, the group also encourages studies of the effects and impact of running on different aspects of life. Members receive an excellent quarterly newsletter, *Fifty-Plus Bulletin*, and participate in continuing studies and surveys. Contact: Fifty-Plus Fitness Association, PO Box 20230, Stanford, California 94309.

Road Runners Club of America has over 450 local affiliates throughout the country. The popular "Run For Your Life" program, a physical fitness program, originated with this group. For brochures and information on their programs and services contact: RRCA National Office, 1150 South Washington, Suite 250, Alexandria, VA 22314. E-mail: execdir@rrca.org. Tel: (703) 836-0558.

Another organization that promotes running is the American Running and Fitness Association www.

americanrunning.org. Write them for information at:
4405 East West Highway, Suite 405, Bethesda, Maryland
20814. Or call: 301-913-9517 or 800-776-2732.

Take Yourself Out to the Ball Game

Baseball is another popular senior sport enjoyed
by over 200,000 people. The National Association of
Senior Citizens Softball promotes international
interest in the game and sponsors teams throughout
the country. Members receive a quarterly newsletter
and have the opportunity of playing in a yearly
national tournament and exhibition games and tournaments around the world. For information write:
National Association of Senior Citizen Softball, Box
1085, Mt. Clemens, MI 48046.

If you are not a participator, but love baseball,
many of the major and minor league baseball teams
offer senior discount days and reduced priced tickets
for clubs. Check with the group ticket office of your
local baseball team for these special offers.

The Amateur Softball Association www.softball.
org provides information on local leagues and how
to start up a softball league. They also coordinate
tournaments for 55+ league players. Contact them
at: 800-44-COACH.

If You're on a Roll, Bowl

Bowling is another great sport for seniors and has
grown tremendously over the past decade. Senior
leagues and tournaments are very popular, and most

bowling alleys reduce game fees for both individuals and groups. Also, since bowling alleys are usually less crowded during the daytime hours, this is one of the best times for senior bowling. The American Bowling Congress www.abcbowling.com, ABC, Bowling Headquarters, 5301 South 76th Street, Greendale, WI 53129 will send you information on bowling for older adults and where there are leagues in your area. Contact: Rick & Diane Gonzalez Webmasters, ABC Tournament Web Site. E-mail: webmaster@abcbowling.com.

If your local bowling alley is a member of the American Bowling Congress www.bowl.com or the Women's International Bowling Congress, you can ask them to send you the 12-part "Bowling for Seniors" packet, which contains ideas on starting leagues, scoring, tournaments, bowling film rentals, and other ideas on developing an active senior program. Or contact your neighborhood bowling center about joining their senior leagues.

Walk for Health

Probably the fastest growing active sport for older adults today is walking. The number of exercise walkers 55+ has more than doubled in recent years, from approximately 8.6 million in 1985 to more than 20 million. Not only is walking good for the heart, but it has also been established that it's good for the bones as well. A recent study found that through a regular schedule of walking, jogging, or climbing stairs, men and women can build stronger bones and help prevent osteoporosis, a disease prevalent in older adults, especially women. Women who exercise regularly can actually increase bone mass in the spine, helping give bones strength and resistance to fracture. The study also found that the typical serious walker is a 53-year old woman who walks an average of 15 miles a week.

Walking programs, clinics, and clubs can be found in almost every town and city in the country. Indoor shopping malls have become popular places to walk (after a walk around the block or the park) because of their safe environment and year-round availability, regardless of weather conditions. In addition, some organized clubs sponsor lectures on a wide range of health topics given by physicians and health professionals. From Walk-A-Dillies to Senior Strutters, there are community groups for walking in your area. Check with local senior citizen groups, "senior" newspapers, community centers and medical facilities to locate a walking club or program in your area.

The Walkers Club of America, a national organization that promotes fitness through walking, will send you a free list of walking clinics and clubs by enclosing a SASE (self-addressed stamped envelope) to: The Walkers Club of America, Box M, Livingston Manor, NY 12758.

If mall walking or marching outside on a bright spring day are your idea of exercise, write for a free walking tip sheet from *The Walking Magazine*. Write: Walking Tip Sheet, 45 Broomfield St., 8th Floor, Boston, MA 02108.

You can also contact the National Association of Mall Walkers, PO Box 191, Hermann, MO 65041, or Walkways Center, 1400 16th Street, NW, Washington, DC 20036 for information on their organizations.

If you live in San Francisco contact: The Walka-block Club of San Francisco. 800-721-7126. Web site: www.walkablock.com.

If you live in New York, check out The New York Walkers Club: Manhattan. Every Saturday, at 9:30 AM in Central Park near the 90th Street and 5th Avenue entrance. Look for their banner. Clinic/workouts last for about 75 minutes. For beginner, intermediate, advanced healthwalkers, racewalkers.

In Queens the group meets Saturdays at 9:00 AM at the Victory Field track, Myrtle Avenue and Woodhaven Boulevard. Warm-ups and cool-downs are at the track and workouts are on the track and on the adjacent Forest Park roadway. For beginners and intermediates.

In Long Island, walkers meet every Saturday at 8:00 AM at Eisenhower Park, East Meadow in front of the Fieldhouse adjacent to the tennis courts at Parking Field 2. Use Hempstead Turnpike Entrance. Clinic/workout last about 75 min. For beginner, intermediate, advanced healthwalkers, racewalkers.

In Vermont check out Country Walkers www.countrywalkers.com. Waterbury, Vermont. 800-464-9255 / 802-244-1387.

World Wide Walkers www.worldwidewalkers. com specializes in creating customized adventure travel tours for individuals and groups.

The Rockport Walking Institute offers a free walking brochure, "The Rockport Guide to Fitness Walking." The brochure contains a self-administered fitness assessment and a 20-week walking program designed for various fitness levels and ages. Call 800-ROCKPORT and ask for the Rockport Fitness Walking Institute.

For those who would like to learn more about the sport of race-walking, send a SASE to Bruce Douglass, Race-walking Chairman, The Athletics Congress, PO Box 120, Indianapolis, IN 46206. They will send back a free directory of race-walking clubs and information on the sport.

If you want to commit serious outside time to walking, you can go to the Sparta Health Spa and Fitness Center in the Catskill Forest Preserve, a 100-acre camp for walkers. For information write: Sparta Health Spa, Box M, Livingston Manor, NY 12758.

Finally, there are several good books and pamphlets available on walking including:

The Rockport Walking Program, by James Rippe, M.D. and Ann Ward, Ph.D., published by Prentice-Hall.

Fitness Walking for Women, by Anne Kashiwa and James Rippe, M. D., Putnam Publishing Group.

Race-walk to Fitness, by Howard Jacobson, available through Walkers Club of America Press, Box M, Livingston Manor, NY 12758.

The Classic Game of Golf

Although seniors have been aware of it for decades, the game of golf has enjoyed an international resurgence, in part due to the tremendous popularity it found among the Japanese during the '80s and '90s. In the United States, the game has grown in popularity because of charismatic golf champions like Tiger Woods. Most public and many private golf courses will give a discount on greens fees for seniors over 65.

The Golf Card www.golfcard.com, which costs $75 a year for single membership and $120 for a couple, was designed especially with seniors in mind. It entitles members to play two free rounds of 18-hole golf at nearly 1,650 member golf courses around the world. As a Golf Card bearer, you also receive *Golf Traveler* magazine, a directory and guide to member courses and resorts participating in the program, as well as discounts on golf vacation packages at nearly 400 member resorts. There is no minimum age requirement to join the program, however the average age of members is 61. Contact: Golf Card International, 64 Inverness Drive E, Englewood, CO 80112. 800-321-8269.

The Pacific Amateur Gold Association (PAGA) offers golfing tours that also include sightseeing. They are called "golferama carousels" because you can take all or part of the tours. There are also activities for the non-golfing partners while the golfers are playing. Tours include the Pacific Northwest North, Pacific Northwest South, Colorful Colorado, Rockies to Remember, New Mexico, and Eastern Canada. Seniors receive a discount on tour packages. For more information write: PAGA, 426 E. Dartmouth Road, Burbank, CA 91504.

Many senior golf competitions and tournaments are held by public and private organizations and clubs throughout the year. Charities have found that sponsoring senior golf tournaments is a great way to raise funds and enlist older adults in a healthy, fun activity. Many regular tournaments advertise special senior discounts for daily or multi-day passes. For instance, daily ground passes for the weeklong Los Angeles Open Golf Tournament cost $15 per day. Senior passes are $10 per day, adding up to some good savings if you plan to attend several days. Check with public golf courses, Departments of Parks and Recreation, and senior publications for their local activities, tournaments, and senior discounts.

You're Never Too Old to Ski
Skiing is a very popular sport among older adults, and there are several clubs and discounts specifically targeted for this age group. For those taking up the sport for the first time, or for veteran skiers who have been schussing down the slopes for decades, with great deals available for seniors, this may be the best

time of all to enjoy this exciting sport. Here are some clubs and organization you should contact:

The Over The Hill Gang www.skiersover50.com. This group (its motto: "Once you're over the hill, you pick up speed") originated with a group of older skiers looking for other older skiers to ski with. They are now an international skiing group with over 6,500 members in all 50 states and 13 countries. They accept members starting at age 50, and promise major discounts. Members not affiliated with local groups can obtain lifetime memberships for $285 (for members over 63) and $425 (for members 50 to 63); most group members pay $100 for three years, $40 for one year, and join periodic ski tours with the group (they also go on sporting-type summer trips). They also offer a yearly Senior Ski Week that takes place at a ski resort in the Rockies or Europe and week-long vacation packages at several resorts around Lake Tahoe, California. Local Gang groups also organize ski trips with their own members or meet to ski weekly at local ski resorts. For information on membership write: Over the Hill Gang International, 1820 West Colorado Avenue, Colorado Springs, CO 80904, or call 719-389-0022.

70+ Ski Club. If you can prove you are over 70, you can join the 70+Ski Club, founded by the remarkable Lloyd Lambert, who skied up until his death at the age of 96. The group now boasts over 3,000 members. One of the original purposes of this group was to make skiing more affordable for older adults on fixed or limited retirement incomes. Club members meet as a group every year for an annual meeting and participate in the 70+ Ski Races at Hunter Mountain in the Catskills. Cost of a lifetime membership is $10, and includes a newsletter and list of ski areas across the country offering free or discounted skiing for seniors. For information write directly to Lloyd's son Richard, who personally registers new members: 1633 Albany Street, Schenectady, NY 12304. 518-346-5505. E-mail: rtl70plus@aol.com

If you ski in the east, there are several ski clubs organized for older adults:

- The Bromley Senior Skiers Club, Bromley Mountain, Box 1130, Manchester Center, VT 05255.

- Mount Snow Senior Ski, Mt. Snow, VT 05356.

- Stratton Senior Skiers Association, c/o Vermont Ski Areas Association, Box 368, Montpelier, VT 05602.

- Waterville Valley Siler Streaks, Stratton Senior Skiers, Stratton Mountain, VT 05155.

- Get Off Your Rockers is an activities club for seniors based in San Diego that provides several ski trips each year to Mammoth and out of state. Contact: GOYR, 11496 Ballybunion Square, San Diego, CA 92128 or call 619-674-GOYR.

Ski resorts throughout the country offer older adults discounts on tickets, rentals, and other amenities. Many discounts range from 50 percent off lift tickets to free tickets and season passes for adults over 55. For example, 46 ski areas or resorts in Michigan offer free downhill or cross-country skiing to people over 55. If you are thinking of taking a ski vacation, check the discounts on vacation packages at hotels and ski lodges associated with the ski area's operators. Always ask about the senior discounts before purchasing daily lift tickets or tickets included with tours and vacation packages.

Even if you don't ski, how about taking the grandchildren on a ski vacation, sharing in the fun and action, and perhaps taking a lesson as well? Weekdays are often slow times at ski resorts, and many offer midweek family plans at greatly reduced rates, often including free lodging (and sometimes lift passes) for the kids.

Cross-Country Skiing

Cross-country skiing is another popular form of exercise that provides an excellent aerobic workout, yet takes it easy on the joints. More than 6.5 million Americans enjoy this sport, which not only costs considerably less than downhill skiing, but also avoids annoying waits in long lift lines. Although many people believe that, "if you can walk, you can cross-country ski," it's not as simple as that. The Cross County Ski Areas Association recommends that everyone take a lesson or two to become familiar with the equipment and techniques. The CCSAA has a $2 directory called "Destinations" that lists more than 200 cross-country ski areas, many of which offer discounts for seniors. To order write: Cross Country Ski Areas Association, 259 Bolton Road, Winchester, NH 03470. Web site: www.xcski.org.

For serious cross-country skiers, the World Master Crosscountry Ski Association sponsors yearly international races. Participants must be over 30, and events are separated into five-year age groups up to 75+. For information contact: World Masters Cross-Country Ski Association USA, 332 Iowa Avenue, PO Box 718, Hayward, WI 54843.

In addition to asking for senior discounts at the more than 800 cross-country ski areas around the country, there are a variety of special packages offered by travel companies. A few include:

The Aspen Skiing Company's programs for skiers over 50 called The Fit for Life 50/Plus program. Call 970-920-1220 for details.

Outdoor Vacations for Women Over 40 offers cross-country ski clinics, weekend and longer packages for women who like adventurous outdoor vacations. Write: Women Over 40, PO Box 200, Groton, MA 01450.

Elderhostel combines its educational programs with low-cost cross-country ski vacations near its educational sites. For information write: Elderhostel, 80 Boylston St., Suite 400, Boston, MA 02116.

Waterville Valley, a New Hampshire Ski area has a cross-country ski package, the Old-Fashioned Winter

Getaway, for skiers over 55. This is a complete week-end package including most meals, wine and cheese party, cross-country classes, a sleigh ride, morning stretch classes, and a guided ski tour with picnic lunch. Call the Waterville Valley Lodging Bureau at (603) 236-8311. Web site: www.neweng landski.com.

Dancing

Dancing is by far the most popular social exercise enjoyed by older adults. It is fun, non-stressing, friendly, and good for you. Look in the activities section of your local newspaper or "senior" newspaper and you will most likely find a senior dance event happening that same week. One Southern California senior citizen newspaper listed no fewer than 12 dance events. Weekly dances and dance classes are held at recreation centers, senior clubs, churches, and community centers.

Swing Dancing has become very popular with seniors. Check out this web site: www.seniors-swing-dance.com.

Stay in Shape with Swimming

Swimming is often recommended for people with arthritis and back or leg injuries. Some fitness experts consider it the healthiest and best overall sport and all-around conditioner. In addition, swimming is one of the most injury-free sports because there is less stress on the joints and muscle system. It is also an inexpensive sport that does not require a lot of special equipment or training.

Swimming is so good for you, in fact, it has been the most popular participation sport in the United States for the past several years. For information on pool locations, lap times and classes contact your health club, YMCA, YWCA, local college, or city Parks and Recreation Department.

Volkssporting

The American Volkssport Association www.ava. org is a nonprofit, volunteer organization whose goal is to promote physical fitness and good health by encouraging all people, regardless of age, to exercise in noncompetitive, stress-free programs. Volkssports are organized, noncompetitive walking, swimming, bicycling and cross-country skiing events. Each event has a premarked scenic trail and/or measured distance designed to appeal to all ages. There are even special provisions for the handicapped to participate in most events. Participation is free of charge.

Volkssporting is an especially beneficial opportunity for seniors who cannot, should not, or simply don't want to exercise in timed or competitive events. Seniors have an equal chance to participate in programs of exercise and fun where no special training or equipment is required and at the same time is safe. Participants in the Lifesports program choose the sport(s), the distance(s), and the pace.

The American Volkssport Association has over 600 member clubs chartered in 49 states. The AVA publishes *The American Wanderer*, a bimonthly newsletter of Volkssporting news, calendar of events, AVA club list, and other information. For information write: American Volkssport Association, 1001 Pat Booker Road, Suite 101, Universal City, TX 78148.

Non-Stress Exercise

Not everyone is able to join in the sports and activities described in these last few pages. However, almost everyone can exercise in some way. Arthritis, one of the most common villains in the battle against growing older, limits millions from participating in the more vigorous, active sports. Range-of-motion exercises (for flexibility and range of movement), stretching, and strength-building programs are enthusiastically supported by the medical community for those having any of the more than 100 different rheumatic disorders. Here are some worthwhile organizations to look into:

The Arthritis Foundation www.arthritis.org has over 70 chapters throughout the country that offer free educational courses, exercise programs, and support resources. They also publish an exercise brochure filled with safety tips and examples of safe, range-of-motion exercises. For information contact: The Arthritis Foundation, 1330 West Peachtree St, Atlanta, Georgia 30309, (404) 872-7100.

The American Physical Therapy Association www.apta.org will send you a free guide sheet with stretching tips to avoid some of the stiffness and minor pain associated with exercise and sports. Send for "Guidelines for Greater Enjoyment of an Active Life,"

Public Relations Dept., American Physical Therapy Association, 1111 No. Fairfax St., Alexandria, VA 22314.

"The Fitness Challenge . . . In Later Years" is a guide outlining an exercise program for maintaining youthful health and energy and suggests ways of enhancing the enjoyment of leisure. For a copy write: U.S. Dept. of Health and Human Services, Commissioner on Aging, 200 Independence Ave. SW, Washington, DC 20201.

The National Institute on Aging www.nih.gov/ nia has articles and other general information on how exercise can help you live a longer, healthier life. Contact: the National Institute on Aging Information Center, PO Box 8057, Gaithersburg, MD 20898-8057. 800-222-2225.

Once you've finished all that terrific exercise that's keeping you fit and healthy, you might want a nice soothing massage to help relax those muscles you've worked so hard. The American Massage Therapy Association www.amtamassage.org will send you a free booklet, "A Guide to Massage Therapy in America." Write them at AMTA, 1130 W. North Shore Ave., Chicago, IL 60626.

CHAPTER 3

"Time of Your Life" Travel

Welcome to the world of senior travel! Today's mature adults have more freedom to travel without the restrictions and responsibilities of supporting children, busy households, complicated schedules, and building careers.

Traveling can be a learning experience, an adventure, a much deserved chance to relax, a physical challenge, or whatever you dream it to be. After waiting this many years, you can be flexible and travel wherever you want, as long as you want, and whenever you want. This translates into lots of savings because, in addition to year-round senior discounts, you can make your travel plans during those times when airline, hotel, car rental, cruise, etc., prices are at their lowest. By using the methods outlined in this chapter, you can save as much as 85 percent on fares and accommodations. Exotic island winter trips, distant European holidays, and cross-country visits to see the grandchildren are just a few of the possibilities. The "trip of a lifetime" can come more than once for mature adults who take advantage of the opportunities available to them.

Travel is the number one desire and activity of the 50+ age group. In fact, 80 percent of all pleasure travel is by individuals over 50. In addition, they take more trips per year, travel longer distances, and spend more time away from home than any other age group.

Every recent study has shown that the overwhelming bulk of all travel expenditures are made by people 50 years of age and over; the young have far less money and less time to travel. And within that 50-plus age group, the segment composed of persons 65 and older is growing faster than any other. Today's mature Americans remain vital and active for many more years than was formerly the case, and they want to travel.

As a result, seniors spend more money, on the whole, than anyone else. The travel industry has vigorously courted the mature adult market by creating numerous discount programs, tours, packages, etc., just for them. Travel agents, airlines, cruise lines, hotels, and other travel businesses know mature adults are free to travel at off-peak times or whenever they desire a change of scenery. They also know that this age group includes shrewd, experienced travelers who look for the best deals to the best places.

The travel industry has also reduced the burden of planning vacations by creating an array of choices and ways to travel, thus relieving seniors of the tedious details of "do it yourself" vacations. Even if you are an experienced traveler, planning a trip can become quite complicated. Yes, there are many excellent, money saving deals available, but rates, fares, and privileges can change at a moments notice. There are such a variety of fares and accommodations, it's often difficult to know if you are really getting the most for your money. It's important to be as thorough as possible in checking out current prices.

Traveling for Free

There are several ways mature adults can take advantage of the little-known "tricks of the trade" within the travel industry to earn free travel. Most free travel requires no special skills, credentials, or contacts. And it can be as luxurious and pleasurable as the most expensive paid vacation. Consider the following if you want to see the world and do it at somebody else's expense:

- Become a tour escort for a travel agency that operates tours; a senior citizen center or clubs with tour programs; or a professional tour operator. Tour operators are always looking for interesting people to lead their tours, especially during the summer tourist season. You will act as tour leader/manager for the group with all your expenses paid. If you are fluent in one or more languages, your services will be especially desirable for tours to foreign countries.

- Organize your own tour or group. If you can enlist enough people, you can get a whole trip, long or short, for free. Some travel agencies recruit teachers who receive a free trip if they bring six students. With 12 students, your spouse can join you for free. Traveling free as a teacher is a very popular way to visit places that would otherwise be financially prohibitive.

• Work for a travel agency. By becoming trained as a travel agent you can qualify for large travel discounts and free travel. Travel agents can often work part-time or from home and still receive the same benefits as full-time counselors.

• Organize a "special interest" tour. If you are a wine aficionado, you might organize a trip to the French wine country; or put together a group from your church for a religious pilgrimage to a Holy Land; or travel to Vienna and Salzburg with other opera buffs for the yearly music festival. Special-interest trips focus on everything from golf, tennis, and bicycling to photography, archaeology, history, theater, music, and gourmet food. A good travel agent can create a tour around your group's common interest. And by organizing and providing the travelers, you will earn a free trip.

• Travel free as a travel writer. If you like to travel and have a flair for writing, you have a good chance of paying for your travels by selling your experiences, short stories, photos, etc., to publications and newspapers that are looking for a new point of view about a different place. Nearly every mature adult publication and dozens of consumer magazines and newspapers can use feature stories, photo spreads and columns on travel, since it is one of the most popular topics of interest to readers.

- Become an air courier. An air courier is someone who accompanies freight (usually small parcels and envelopes filled with documents), which has been checked as baggage on a flight. In the case of foreign flights, the package arrives with the courier and is processed through customs immediately along with the courier's other bags rather than remaining in a warehouse waiting customs clearance. Courier companies offer assignments to the general public in exchange for free or deeply discounted tickets (50 percent or more). The key to becoming a courier is being flexible and able to travel light. Courier firms want their representatives to maintain a well-dressed, respectable image and welcome responsible mature people they can rely on.

- Buy a new automobile overseas. Several European delivery specialists will pay your round-trip airfare if you buy an automobile from and pick it up overseas. They also arrange necessary customs and vehicle inspections once the car arrives in the United States. You can save from $4,000 to $7,000 on a new Jaguar, BMW, Mercedes, Volvo, Saab, Porsche, Audi, Volkswagen, etc., by arranging European delivery.

- Become a lecturer, performer, or organizer aboard a cruise ship. You can cruise free as an expert on a specific subject, business, or other interesting field. Historians, anthropologists, financial experts, naturalists, former athletes, coaches, musicians, cosmetologists, writers, entertainers, retired executives, CEOs, teachers, etc. are always in high demand to provide guests with an entertaining and interesting array of information and activities. Your job would be to present a series of lectures, organize activities, etc., and be available for informal demonstrations and discussions. In return you receive an all expenses paid cruise.

Home Exchange

A great way to stretch your travel dollars is to participate in a home exchange program. There are several books, clubs and exchange services that list thousands of homes around the world whose owners offer club members a free stay for a week or more. The International Home Exchange Service publishes three directories a year with more than 7,000 listings and details on how to set up an exchange. More than 80 percent of the listings are from outside the United States, ranging as far away as Brazil, Nepal, Australia and Zimbabwe, but most of the exchange homes are in Europe. Subscriptions are $55 per year. For information contact: Book Passage, 800-999-7909 or International Home Exchange Service, 415-956-1011. Web site: www.bookpassage.com. E-mail: message@ bookpassage.com.

www.homexchange.com charges a very low $30 per year (which is less than the leading "seniors" home exchange service).

Home Base Holidays www.homebase-hols.com/. Operated in an alliance of established home exchange agencies worldwide to ensure members have a wide choice of quality listings in several countries.

Israel House Exchange www.jewishtravel.com/community/exchange.html. Free service of Jewish Travel. Offers postings of home swapping opportunities.

National House Exchange www.national-house-exchange.co.uk/. Mutual house Exchanges throughout England, Scotland, Wales, Northern Ireland and Republic of Ireland.

Vacation Homes Unlimited www.vacation-homes.com/ offers home exchange listings to members.

House-Sitting

If you like the idea of a free place to stay, consider becoming a professional house-sitter. This is one way to enjoy beautifully furnished (sometimes including maid-service) homes and mansions for free. Most people would rather not abandon their pets to a strange kennel or leave their houses vacant while they travel. A professional house-sitter can spend nearly all year helping different folks out by watching their houses and pets, usually getting paid for it. Free house-sitting works in the opposite way as well. People who own expensive vacation and resort homes often visit these homes only once or twice a year. They also want the peace of mind of having their homes watched over and cared for while they are not there. When they arrive for their vacation, you can visit friends or relatives while they are vacationing in "your" home. How does year-round living in Key West, Florida; Kannapali Beach, Maui; Aspen, Colorado or Malibu, California sound? Many people have homes in the Bahamas, Mexico and other foreign countries that they prefer be lived in year-round.

Another way to live and travel for free is by house-sitting for homes that are for sale. Houses built for "spec" and model homes especially are perfect for house-sitting. Higher priced homes often stay on the market for several months at a time. Meanwhile, you are enjoying a brand new home. Older homes up for sale are often left empty because their owners have already moved into new homes. Fine homes with swimming pools, tennis courts and lush gardens need someone to watch over them so vandals don't take advantage of their being empty for long periods of time.

Planning Trips and Using Travel Agencies

The simplest and best place to start planning a trip is with a professional travel agency. Choose one that is a member of the American Society of Travel Agents (ASTA) www.astanet.com. Most services and counseling provided by travel agents is free of charge.

Agents make their money from commissions paid by airlines or other travel businesses.

You can choose a travel agency that specializes in a particular type of travel or travel to a specific geographic area. There are agencies that specialize in cruises, general pleasure travel, or business travel. Some handle groups and tours while others work only with individual travelers.

ASTA has senior memberships, for those travel professionals who have been an ASTA member (with ASTA membership in their name) for more than 12 years. Annual dues are $50. Contact ASTA at: 1101 King St, STE 200, Alexandria, VA 22314. Attention: Pamela Massey, Membership Sales.703-739-2782 or 800-440-2782. E-mail: Pamelam@astahq.com.

Ask yourself these questions when choosing a travel agent:
- Are your personal travel requests considered by the agent, such as first- or ground-floor accommodations, in-room amenities, smoking or nonsmoking seats and hotel rooms, and bellman to carry heavy luggage?
- When discussing budgets, are you asked about your flexibility in making travel arrangements?
- Are you asked about health concerns?
- Will your travel agent follow through on your behalf, especially if a problem arises during you trip?

If the answers to these questions are "yes," then you have found a good agency for your travel plans.

You can help your agent by making a list of the kinds of activities, recreation, and accommodations you prefer. Also make a rough budget of what you expect to spend and save. If you hate traveling in groups or you don't want to spend more than $60 for dinner, or you prefer to shop rather than sightsee, list those desires as well. Take travel brochures from the agency to help you. Travel agents can advance-book everything from hotel reservations and transportation, to theater tickets and dinner reservations. Working closely with them will assure you of a smooth-running, well-planned trip.

Should you plan your trip yourself? Since fares and rates sometimes change daily, a travel agency's sophisticated computer system linked to thousands of current prices, gives them the advantage by having this information at their fingertips. If you are planning a complex trip including many stops, I suggest using a professional travel agent. A recent survey of New York City travel agents showed that prices quoted for the lowest airfare to other cities varied more than 50 percent. Some travel agents quote the first price they see and don't bother to find out about the bargains. This shows how important it is to establish a working relationship with a single travel agent who will be more inclined to spend time on your travel needs.

Contact the following to help in your search:

American Society of Travel Agents (ASTA) www.astanet.com. World Headquarters: 1101 King Street Alexandria, VA 22314. 703-739-2782 or 800-440-2782. E-mail: pamelam@astahq.com.

Ask if there are any additional charges for arranging a trip. Some agencies bill clients for long distance phone calls, faxes, or other services. Also, always ask about any restrictions or cancellation fees which may apply to your tickets or reservations. Finally, be sure to let your agent know from the beginning that you are a mature adult and, as such, are entitled to all senior discounts available.

Doing It Yourself

If you decide to plan your own trip always ask for the "senior citizen discount" when making your reservations, at the time of purchase or before you check-in. If you wait until you pick up your tickets or check out, it might be too late. Some hotels do not give a senior citizen discount if reservations are booked through a travel agent because they are paying two discounts, a 10 percent travel agent's commission and a 10 percent (or more) senior citizen discount. Also, be aware that you can save money by using toll-free numbers to reserve hotel rooms in hundreds of destinations. Call 800-555-1212 to obtain toll-free numbers.

Some discounts may apply only between certain hours, on certain days of the week, or during specific seasons of the year. Check this out before making reservations.

Don't always take the over-50 discount without inquiring about other available rates. Sometimes special promotional discounts, available to anybody at any age, turn out to have better savings. Ask the reservationist or ticket seller to find you the lowest possible rate at that time.

Since many mature adults look younger than their chronological age, it is particularly important to carry identification with your proof of age (driver's license, passport, resident alien card, Medicare card, senior I.D. card, birth certificate) or membership in an over-50 organization such as AARP or Mature Outlook.

If you want to try your luck with online booking and auctions look up these sites and compare their different programs, pricing structure and ease of use:

Expedia www.expedia.msn.com.

Travelocity www.travelocity.com.

Travelscape.com www.travelscape.com.

Travel.com www.ontravel.com.

PriceLine www.priceline.com.

Bid4Travel www.bid4travel.com.

EBay www.ebay.com.

Going Going Gone www.goinggoinggone.com/going/homego.htm.

SkyAuction.com www.skyauction.com.

Yahoo Auctions auctions.yahoo.com.

Cheap Tickets www.cheaptickets.com. Cheap tickets started as America's travel store in 1986. They specialize in low fare and discount airline tickets and provide millions of discount tickets. Their tickets are for regularly scheduled flights, out of all major airports in the United States, Europe, Asia and South America, and on all major airlines. Now you can search for cheap tickets online, 24-hours a day. The search is free to registered users.

Travel Agencies, Clubs and Organizations for 50+ Travelers

Some travel agencies and organizations cater solely to mature travelers. They offer trips and vacations for the fiercely independent or those who enjoy the companionship of tour groups. There are so many choices for the mature traveler today that the only problem is making a decision on where to go.

Tip: Remember to check your tour brochure carefully to see whether tipping for local guides and bus drivers is included in the cost of your vacation package. It is customary to tip the tour director at the end of your tour. Depending on the person's performance, $1-$3 per day per traveler is sufficient.

Experienced Travel Companies

1-2 Cruise. 11310 West Grant, Wichita, KS 67209. 800-866-3879.

The Cruise Connection. 624 Brandon Avenue, Springfield, Virginia 22150. 703-451-2010.

Grand Circle Travel www.gct.com. Grand Circle Travel, Inc., 347 Congress St., Boston, MA 02210. 617-350-7500; 800-248-3737, is the oldest of the U.S. firms dealing only with senior citizens (quarterly magazine, *Pen Pal*, and travel-partner service). In business for more than 40 years, it enjoys a large and loyal following who respond especially to offers of extended-stay vacations in off-season months, and to low-cost foreign areas with mild climates. The greater number of Grand Circle's passengers are those spending 2 to 20 weeks on the Mediterranean coast of Spain, in a seaside kitchenette apartment supplied with utensils, china, and cutlery.

Others go for several weeks to Portugal and Madeira, the Canary Islands, and the Balearics. The tour company states that older Americans can enjoy a "full season" at these exotic locations for not much more than they'd spend to go to Florida or other domestic havens.

While neither Spain nor Portugal offers swimming weather in winter, their low prices enable seniors (even those living mainly on Social Security) to vacation in dignity, enjoying good-quality meals and modern apartments in place of the fast-food outlets and shabby motels to which they're often relegated here at home. Grand Circle's extended stays are supplemented by nearly a dozen other programs: Alaskan cruises, European and Asian River cruises, hiking and biking holidays, Canadian holidays, inexpensive homestays, tours to Europe, India, Africa and the Orient-booked by thousands, but not yet as popular as those "stay-put" vacations for several weeks in a balmy, foreign clime.

The Alternatives to Solitude

If you are a mature single, you don't have to travel alone. By simply mailing $5 for a membership in the Grand Circle Travel Club, operated by Grand Circle Travel, Inc., you can obtain the names of potential companions for your next trip. The club distributes quarterly magazines with "Pen Pal" features listing dozens of applications by mature singles for travel partners. These, in effect, are "travel personals," but proper to a fault, and fascinating to read as they detail the varied goals of the mature, experienced travelers submitting them. See their web site at www.gct.com/html/home.htm.

Elderhostle. 75 Federal St., Boston, MA 02110. 617-426-7788. Elderhostel is the much-discussed, increasingly-popular, nonprofit group that works with 2,000 U.S. and foreign educational institutions to provide seniors 55 and over with residential study courses at unbeatable costs: $450 per week for room, board, and instruction and field trips (but not including air fare) in the U.S. and Canada; an average of $3,300 for three weeks abroad, this time including air fare. Accommodations and meals are in student residence halls, underused youth hostels or standard motels and hotels. Web site: www.elderhostel.org.

Partners-In-Travel. 11660 Chenault St., #219, Los Angeles, CA 90049. 310-476-4869. Offers a free booklet on traveling cheaper solo. Long in business, they are an able company.

Mayflower Tours. 1225 Warren Avenue, Downers Grove, IL. 60515. 630-435-8500, 800-323-7604. Mayflower targets mature travelers 55 or over by offering leisurely paced, fully escorted trips including tours to Hawaii, the Canadian Rockies, and Georgia's Golden Isles. Special trips allow grandparents and grandchildren to travel together. Participants travel by air conditioned motorcoach, stay in quality hotels, and eat meals with others in the tour. If you are a single traveler, Mayflower will find you a roommate as long as you make your reservations 30 days in advance. Web site: www.mayflowertours.com.

Saga International Holidays, Ltd. Saga Holidays, 222 Berkeley Street, Boston, MA 02116. 617-262-2262 or toll free 800-343-0273 outside Massachusetts; or visit their web site at www.sagaholidays.com. Contact: Jill Whitney, Customer Commitment Department.

Saga sends over 250,000 senior citizens on vacation each year. To tap into that major movement (and the bargaining power it represents), the U.S. organization routes many of its trans-Atlantic tours through London, then combines its older American travelers into one group with older British and Australian passengers. Such blending of English-speaking nationalities adds "zip" to any tour.

Saga's major stock-in-trade is escorted motor-coach tours: heavily (and throughout the year) within the United States, heavily in Europe, but also in Mexico, in Australia and the Far East, and in South America. Although it also offers cruises and extended stays, it is the escorted motorcoach, competitively-priced, that most of its clients demand. Recently, an ingenious "Road Scholar" plan of serious lectures delivered en route has added more than the usual content to several popular motorcoach itineraries.

Saga specializes in making travel plans for people over 50. Trips can be booked through direct mail or telephone only, since there are no travel agents representing them in this country. Saga has become very popular with American travelers because of the opportunities they offer for traveling with mature adults from other countries such as Great Britain and Australia. A three-year membership costs $5. Members receive travel discounts, a bi-monthly magazine called *Connections*, opportunities for social gatherings, and a list of "Penfriends" and "Partnership" to help find travel companions and meet people through the mail.

Solo Flights. 10 Taits Mill Road, Trumbull, CT 06611. 800-266-1566; 203-445-0107. Geared to single mature audiences. Free newsletter describing tours.

YMT Vacations, Inc. ("Your Man Tours"). 8831 Aviation Boulevard, Inglewood, California 90301. 800-922-9000; 310-649-3820; fax: 310-649-2118. Web site: www.ymtvacations.com. YMT, 32 years in business, operates almost solely in the United States, though it has recently branched out with tours to the Caribbean and Panama Canal. Its tours are fully escorted, and sometimes consist of a mixture of tour modes: a one-week stay in an attractive land location followed by a one-week cruise; a tour by air to all four of the major Hawaiian Islands (from $1499 plus air fare); a cruise of

Alaskan waters, followed by a land tour of Alaska. Of all the senior citizen specialists, YMT is perhaps the least expensive; it offers excellent values, and takes pleasure in attracting cost-conscious seniors to its fully escorted arrangements.

AARP Travel Service. 601 E St NW, Washington DC 20049. 800-303-4222. AARP members have a variety of travel benefits from which to choose. Including escorted tours, trips and cruises to locations all over the globe at discounted group rates. Memberships in AARP cost $8/year and includes the bi-monthly publication *Modern Maturity* and the *AARP News Bulletin*. Minimum age is 50. If you belong to an organization like AARP or Mature Outlook, some of these bargains are yours at age 50. Others come along a little later at varying birthdays, so watch for the cutoff points. In many cases, if the person purchasing the ticket qualifies for the minimum age requirement, others sharing the same accommodations are entitled to the same reduced rates. Web site: www.aarp.org. Email: member@aarp.org.

Where to Stay: Hotel, Motel and Resort Bargains

Today's mature traveler has more choices of accommodations than ever before. Almost anywhere you go you will find a senior discount. Whether you make reservations yourself or through a travel agent, consider the following:

- Hotels, motels, and resorts often offer even better discounts if you belong to a recognized senior organization or discount airline program.

Remember to ask at what age the senior discount begins.

• When calling for reservations know the dates, arrival time, number of people in your party, price range, type and quality of room you prefer (including amenities and extras: nonsmoking rooms, free complimentary breakfasts, health & fitness centers, indoor pools and Jacuzzis, facilities for the handicapped).

• Whenever possible use (800) toll-free numbers to book reservations through a central operator.

• Always ask about the senior citizen discount at the time you make reservations and when you check-in. Hotel/motel discounts range from 10 percent to as high as 50 percent off regular room rates.

• Request a written confirmation or a reservation confirmation number and bring it when you check in. Also consider guaranteeing your reservation by prepaying the first night (either by credit card or check). By doing this, whether you use it or not, you are guaranteed a reservation that will be held for you even if you arrive late.

• Another way to guarantee your reservation is to prepay through a travel voucher from your travel agent. Visa, MasterCard, and other major credit card companies now issue these through travel agents. To use a travel voucher, simply present it when you check in.

Accommodations for today's mature traveler run the range of price and comfort levels. Prices range from $15 up to several hundred dollars a night depending on your preferences. Listed below are examples of national and international lodging organizations offering senior discounts:

Best Western www.bestwestern.com. Best Western has more than 3,300 independently owned hotels, inns and resorts across the United States and abroad. Most of the affiliates offer a 10 percent senior discount if you are 55 or over. AARP members receive a 10 percent discount on room rates. Advance reservations are recommended. Call 800-528-1234.

Budget Host Inns www.budgethost.com. Located across the United States and Canada, this chain of inns offers senior citizen discounts that vary from inn to inn. Write for a free *Budget Host Inn Travel Directory*, which includes coupons, toll free reservation numbers and a listing of all inns: Budget Host Inns, 2601 Jacksboro Highway, Caravan Suite 202, P.O. Box 10656, Fort Worth, Texas 76114 or call 800-283-4678.

Baymont Inns www.baymontinns.com. This inexpensive motel chain offers a 10 percent discount in many of its establishments, if you are over 55. Baymont Inns are located across the South and Midwest in about 32 states with over 190 locations.

Confirm your discount when making reservations. Call 800-428-3438.

Fairmont Hotels (formerly known as Canadian Pacific) www.fairmont.com. Offers special senior citizen discounts at participating hotels. There are 36 locations through the United States and Canada. They also offer special weekend rates. Call 800-828-7447.

Country Hearth Inns www.countryhearth.com. A chain of inexpensive motels that offer a 10 percent discount if you are over 50. Over 45 locations. Call (800) 848-5767 or 800-4-HEARTH. Contact: Carolyn Neal, Coordinator. E-mail: info@countryhearth.com.

Days Inns www.daysinn.com. Days Inns: From 15% to 50% (usually 15%) off at 1,800 participating inns, hotels, and suite-hotels in the United States, Canada, Mexico, the Netherlands and France. They also feature "Day Stops," to members (50 years and older) of their September Days Club; also offer 10% off meals, and discounts on Alamo Car rentals; send $15 to September Days Club, September days memberships are entitled to group rates on trips and escorted tours, discounted prescription drugs, vehicle insurance plan, discounts at theme parks, free luggage tags, information on last-minute travel opportunities and a free subscription to *Golden Years* magazine. 800-344-3636.

Drury Inns www.drury-inn.com. If you are over 50 or a member of AARP, Drury Inns offer 10 percent discounts on regular rooms at all locations. Call 1-800-DRURYINN. Contact: Melissa McNeely. E-mail: MMcNeely@ldd.net.

Embassy Suites Hotels www.embassy-suites.com. Discounts vary for each Embassy hotel. Complimentary breakfast and cocktails are also included. Call 800-EMBASSY (362-2779).

Enjoy Florida www.enjoyflorida.com (formerly known as Karena Hotels). These hotels include certain Ramada and Econolodge Inns located mainly in Florida. AARP discounts vary at each inn. Call 800-365-6935.

Exel Inns Of America, Inc. www.exelinns.com. Located in Michigan, South Dakota, Illinois, Texas, Wisconsin, Minnesota and Iowa, these inns offer a 10 percent senior citizen discount on room rates if you are 55 or over. Call 800-356-8013.

Hampton Inns www.hampton-inn.com (a part of the Hilton). Offers a special membership program for people over 50. The "Lifestyle 50" program entitles guests to share a room with three other travelers 50+ for the one-person rate. The "Lifestyle 50" program is honored at any of the 220 Hampton Inns across the United States. Call 800-HAMPTON (426-7866).

Holiday Inns and Holiday Inn Crowne Plaza Hotels www.holiday-inns.com. Guests 55 and over or members of AARP, receive a 10 percent discount on all room rates at over 1,000 participating hotels. Call 800-HOLIDAY.

Howard Johnson www.howardjohnson.com. Take 15% off for seniors 60 years and older, and 20% off for AARP members, at all of the nation's H.J. hotels. Phone toll free: 800- IGOHOJO.

Hyatt Hotels www.hyatt.com. Age does have its privileges. If you are over 62, you are eligible to save up to 50% off their regular room rates at participating Hyatt hotels and resorts in the continental United States and Canada. In addition, be sure to take advantage of Golden Passport, Hyatt's award-winning frequent flyer guest program. As a Gold Passport member, you can choose to earn either Gold Passport points or airline miles on every stay. Your points can be redeemed for exciting travel awards such as room upgrades, nights at Hyatt or even complete vacations! Plus, on every stay, you will receive membership benefits. To join Gold Passport, visit www.goldpassport.com. For more information, call 800-233-1234.

Inns of America. This chain is located in California, Georgia, and Florida and offers 10 percent discount to guests over 55 or to AARP members. Call 800-826-0778. E-mail: innsamerica@ix.netcom.com.

Knights Inn. A guaranteed 10% discount to persons 50 and over- sometimes it's more than 10%. 250 locations across the United States and Canada. Call 800-758-8999.

La Quinta Inns www.laquinta.com. Offers 10% off to people age 55 and older. Call 800-531-5900.

Marriott Hotels www.marriotthotels.com. At more than 200 Marriott's in the United States, AARP members receive 10% off normal rates, up to 50% off with a 21-day non-refundable advance purchase, and 20% off on food and non-alcoholic beverages. AARP members also receive 10% off at Marriott's Fairfield Inns and Courtyards by Marriott (two subsidiary chains), and 15% off at Marriott's Residence Inns. Phone Marriott itself at 800-228-9290, Courtyard by Marriott at 800-346-4000, Residence Inn at 800-331-3131, and Fairfield Inns at 800-322-4000.

Nendels Motor Inns. Current locations: Washington, Kansas, and Texas. Receive 10 percent off regular room rates if you are 60 or over or a member of a national senior organization. Also locations in the Pacific Northwest. Call 800-547-0106.

Omni Hotels www.omnihotels.com. Fifty locations in the United States offer 10 percent discount on regular room rates to AARP members. Advance reservations suggested. Call 800-843-6664.

Peabody Hotels www.peabodyorlando.com, www.peabodymemphis.com. The Orlando Peabody offers up to 50% off the starting rate, depending on room availability for seniors, with some rates starting at $125. You can also earn United Airline Miles for your stay. Two locations: Orlando, Florida and Memphis, Tennessee.

The Pointe-Mountainside Resorts. These three resorts in Phoenix offer AARP discounts to guests 50 or over. Locations are in Tapatio Cliff, South Mountain and Squaw Peak. Includes breakfast and free cocktail reception. Call 800-8POINTE.

Quality Inns/Comfort Inns/Clarion (Choice Hotels International) www.choicehotels.com. With over 3,000 hotels worldwide, Choice Hotels International offers a year round "Prime Time" program. If you are 60+ or a member of AARP, you are eligible for the Super Saver rate of 10 to 30 percent off the room rate. Call 800-221-2222.

Radisson. Begun in September of 1997, the "Senior Breaks" program allows persons 65 or older to stay at any Radisson Hotel Worldwide (there are 345 in 39 countries) at a discount of 25 to 40% off the regular rate. For more information, call 800-333-3333.

Ramada Inns www.ramada.com. Many (about three-quarters) give the same 25% off to persons 60 and up. Phone toll free 800-2-RAMADA.

Red Lion Inns/Thunderbird Motor Inns. "Our senior citizens are special guests and in addition to offering our routine courtesy and assistance to make your stay a pleasant, enjoyable one, our senior citizens receive a 10% discount off the room rates. Please call 800-233-0827 to reserve a room at Thunderbird Motor Inn."

Red Roof Inns www.redroof.com. Offers a new senior savings program "Redi Card" which entitles members to a 10 percent discount on room rates, plus discounts on future stays at *Red Roof Inns*, a quarterly newsletter, and Rand McNally road map. You can apply for the Redi Card online at www.redroof.com. Over 300 locations across the United States. The Redi card also gives first preference to those applying for non-smoking rooms. Call 800-843-7663.

Sheraton Hotels. Located in over 62 countries, participating Sheraton Hotels offer the standard AARP discount to those over 60. Ask for the discount when making reservations. Though they caution that the discount can be withheld during periods of peak business, and is not applicable to minimum-rate rooms, virtually all Sheratons give a 25% discount to persons 60 and older. Phone toll free 800-325-3535.

Sonesta International Hotels www.sonesta.com. If you are a member of AARP, you will receive a 10 to 15 percent discount off room rates at any of their 13 deluxe hotels. Make sure to request your discount when making reservations. Call 1-800-SONESTA.

Stouffer Hotels (part of Marriot). This hotel chain offers a "Great Years Program" that gives senior citizens

59 and over up to 50 percent discount off regular room rates. Available only at participating Stouffer Hotels. Call 800-HOTELS.

Super 8 Motels, Inc. www.super8.com. Over 1,900 Super 8 Motels across the United States and Canada offer a 10 percent discount for senior travelers 55 or over. Rates vary from hotel to hotel. Call 800-843-1991.

Travelodge and Discount Hotels www.travelodge. com. Participating locations offer a 15 percent discount on room rates to members of most senior organizations. Over 300 locations. Travelodge offers guests $20 gas coupons for $1. You must purchase the Travelodge card to get the discount. This entitles you to 10% off your next two stays at Travelodge. Call 800-255-3050.

Vagabond Inns www.vagabondinns.com. AARP rates vary from 10% to 30% depending on location. 35 locations in California, two in Reno, Nevada and one in Seattle, Washington.

Westin Hotels and Resorts www.westin.com. This luxury hotel chain offers discounts up to 50 percent off regular room rates. Advance reservations are required. Each hotel has its own discount policy.

Tip: *Always* check for a senior citizen discount, even if you are booking into an independently owned establishment. You have nothing to lose by asking, and you may find they offer considerable savings in order to stay competitive with the chain operators.

If You Don't Want to Stay in a Hotel

If you are innovative, imaginative and will consider alternative sources of lodging, the following possibilities can also save you money in your travels.

Two resources to assist you in alternate sources of travel are: www.stay4free.com and www.travel secrets.com.

INNter Lodging. INNter Lodging is a co-op organization. Members stay in a choice of homes across the United States and Canada at very little cost. Member must agree to make their homes available to other travelers at least four months of the year. For information write to INNter Lodging Co-op, Tacoma, Washington 98407; or call 206-756-0343.

Servas www.servas.org. 11 John St., Suite 407, New York, NY 10038. 212-267-0252. E-mail: info@servas. org. SERVAS is an agency that avoids the use of standard hotels and replaces them with a people-friendly form of lodgings. Staying with families while abroad serves the triple purpose of avoiding loneliness, gaining new friendships and insights, and lowering costs. You not only escape from that burdensome single supplement, but start from a radically lower base of costs.

On the eve of a trip, members obtain from Servas the names and addresses of families in every major city who have expressed their willingness to receive other Servas members into their homes (for short stays) free of charge, because they believe in the profound moral aspect of such hospitality. Yearly fee for Servas membership: $65-not including $25 refundable deposit.

Women Welcome Women www.womenwelcome women.org.uk. 88 Easton Street, High Wycombe, Buckinghamshire, HP11 1LT, United Kingdom. Or call 011-44-1494-465441, between 9:30am and 1:30 P.M. (British time). 2,500 members strong, currently in its 15th year of operation. This club was formed to facilitate "cultural exchanges" between women from all parts of the globe. The club also arranges conferences and gatherings where members take courses, hear lectures, sightsee and socialize in the home city of the sponsoring member.

Regular homestays are arranged on a person-to-person basis. A member looks through the organization's directory (sent out annually, it includes the names and addresses of all members), decide where they want to travel, and then contact members in the area to see if they can accommodate them. W.W.W. currently has members in 70 countries, including such exotic locales as Vietnam, Turkey, Zimbabwe, Kuwait and Latvia. There are high concentrations in Europe (particularly Germany, the U.K., the Netherlands, Belgium and Switzerland), Australia, Japan and the U.S. The suggested donation for membership is 20 British pounds (approximately $35 to $40) to defray their cost.

Senior Gateways of Florida. 126 Second Ave. NE, St. Petersburg, FL 33701. 727-896-6640 or toll free 800-223-8123.

YMCAs. The YMCA offers inexpensive accommodations throughout North America that are safe, comfortable, and conveniently located. You should make reservations several months in advance due to their popularity. Included is your room, use of swimming pool, exercise. facilities, and library. Some Y's offer package programs that include breakfast, some other meals, and sightseeing. Write: YMCA, 101 North Wacker Drive, Chicago, Illinois 60606. Call 312-977-0031 to find the YMCA nearest your location.

Auto-Truck Stops. Full-service truck stops offer inexpensive, comfortable hotel rooms. Some include amenities such as laundromats, restaurants, barbershops, and convenience stores. First priority for available rooms is reserved for truckers.

Campus Accommodations. Colleges and universities across the United States, Canada, and Europe rent rooms to travelers in the summertime and during school vacations. The cost is minimal, and some include breakfast and use of campus facilities. Contact the housing office of colleges in areas you plan to visit or get a copy of "U.S. and Worldwide Accommodations Guide." Write to Campus Travel Service, P.O. Box 5007, Laguna Beach, CA 92652 or call 714-497-3044.

Oakwood Resort Apartments. Oakwood Corporate Housing Resort Apartments www.oakwood.com. These resort apartments may be rented by mature travelers 55 and over. They are located in metropolitan areas in California, Nevada, Washington DC, Georgia, Virginia, North Carolina, Texas, and Colorado. They must be rented for 30 days or more, and if rented between November and February, there is a substantial discount. The apartments are completely furnished, including kitchen utensils, and linens. Most locations have tennis courts, fitness centers, swimming pools, and clubhouses. Write to: R&B Enterprises, 2222 Corinth Ave., Los Angeles, CA 90064, or call 800-888-0808.

Camping

According to a survey by the camping industry, the number of campers who are retirees is increasing. And as that number continues to grow, the over-50 crowd will be requiring more conveniences and a greater choice of recreational activities. There are public campgrounds, private campgrounds, primitive, and luxurious resort campgrounds. Many are located near historic points of interest, major attractions or within state and national parks. Prices range from as low as $1.50 to $20 per night. Amenities include fireplaces, picnic tables, flush toilets, showers, electricity, running water, grocery stores, dumping stations, and coin laundries. For information about the National Park System—including Golden Eagle, Golden Age, and Golden Access passports—see the last section of this chapter.

For information about Kampgrounds of America (KOA) www.koakampgrounds.com, the largest chain of privately owned campgrounds in the U.S., send for the KOA Handbook and Directory. Kampgrounds are located in the United States, Canada, Mexico and Japan. Write: Kampgrounds of America, 550 N. 31st Street, 4th Floor, Billings, Montana 59101, or call 1-800-548-7239 or (406) 254-7440, or pick up a directory at your nearest KOA campground.

Another multi-site campground operation is Yogi Bear's Jellystone Park Camp Resorts and Safari Campground in New Hampshire. If you stay at this campground on a site for a non-holiday, full season rate (between June 23–September 4th), you get a 10% discount. If you are vacationing with your family and have grandchildren, they have a special grandparent rate of $2.00 night. Web site: www. yogibearnh.com. E-mail: yogi@jellystonenh.com.

A highly successful international organization, The Good Sam Club www.goodsamclub.com, offers discounts and benefits to owners of recreational vehicles. Although membership is open to all ages, the majority of those belonging are over 50. Over 2,000 local chapters host outings, hold meetings and schedule regular campouts. Savings and services include: 10 percent discount at 1,600 RV parks and campgrounds; 10 percent discounts on RV parts and accessories; Emergency road service (includes towing); RV vehicle insurance; Health insurance; Subscriptions to *Trailer*

Life and *MotorHome* magazines; Trip routing service; Mail forwarding service; Credit card protection; Lost pet service and lost key service.

With all these benefits and a membership fee of $25 a year, The Good Sam Club is a bargain for folks who spend a lot of tune on the road. They also organize "caraventure" tours all over the world. For information: The Good Sam Club, P.O. Box 6888, Englewood, Colorado 80155-6888 call 1-800-234-3450. E-mail: goodsam@tl.com, www.rvnet.com.

RV'ing Women www.rvingwomen.com. P.O. Box 1940, Apache Junction, AZ 85217. 888-55-RVING or 480-983-4678. E-mail: rvingwomen@juno.com. Offers advice, support, seminars, caravans, and a bi-monthly magazine and membership directory to "on-your-own" women RV'ers who are single, widowed, divorced or have husbands who just hate camping. Membership is $42 a year.

Bed and Breakfasts

There are so many wonderful Bed & Breakfast accommodations located in the United States and abroad that it would be impossible to try and list them. For the most current information regarding Bed and Breakfast establishments in areas you plan to visit, contact the tourist agencies in those areas or check your local bookstore or library for Bed and Breakfast directories. The AAA Club Directory for each state also lists and rates Bed and Breakfasts.

Evergreen Bed & Breakfast Club www.evergreen club.com. 201 West Broad Street #181, Falls Church, VA 22046. 800-962-2392. E-mail: travelbb@aol.com.

The Evergreen Bed & Breakfast Club is designed for those mature travelers over 50 willing to give up rooms in their homes to other travelers. Club members provide guest rooms for fellow members traveling throughout the United States, Canada, and Europe. There are presently over 600 homes in the Evergreen Club. Membership costs $50 per couple or $40 for singles. Members receive annual directories and a quarterly newsletter. The directory gives names, addresses, occupations, interests, policies on smoking and pets and a listing of special attractions in the area. Rates are generally under $25 per night.

More Clubs for Mature Travelers

Partners-In-Travel www.partners-in-travel.com. 1407 W. Prien Lake Road, Holly Hill Plaza, Lake Charles, LA 70605. 337-480-0246. E-mail: info@ partners-in-travel.com. Partners-in-Travel, open to all ages, offers single travelers an opportunity to connect with other travelers for friendship and savings on the cost of travel. A $40 annual membership package includes a bimonthly newsletter with free listings for members seeking travel companions, free counseling, free listings of home-exchange, and a special publication, *To Your Good Health*.

Loners on Wheels. 808 Lester St., Poplar Bluff, MO 63901. 573-785-2420. E-mail: lonersonwheels@geocities.

com. Operates for mature singles who possess recreational vehicles. A rather large organization, it forms caravans of RVs operated solely by singles, and takes them to rallies and camp-outs all over the country and occasionally to Mexico, too. Annual dues: $36, plus an enrollment fee of $5 (the first year only).

Loners of America www.napanet/~mbost/index. html. P.O. Box 3314, Napa, California 94558-0331. This is another club for single RVers. There are more than 1,200 members throughout the country, ranging in age from 40s to 90s. They hold campouts, meetings, rallies, and caravans all over the country. Members receive an annual membership directory and newsletter detailing events and activities. Annual dues are $40.

Travel Companion Exchange. P.O. Box 833, Amityville, NY 11701. 800-392-1256. This organization was founded by the well-known travel figure, Jens Jurgen. His is the most elaborate of all travel match-up services, supplying you with literally thousands of available listings, all carefully grouped by computer into helpful categories ("special interests," "special travel plans," and the like) to enable you to make a wise choice. You will find a suitable travel "match-up," Annual fee is $298.

American Jewish Congress www.ajcongress.org. 15 E. 84th Street, New York, NY 10028. 800-221-4694; 212-879-4500. This organization offers tours to Israel for single travelers who join other similarly aged solo travelers. Every year they offer two departures for singles between ages of 39 and 55, and four trips for solo travelers over the age of 55.

Fly and Save Money

Most airlines offer senior citizens discounts of at least 10 percent off regular fares (you can fly first class for free if you can prove you are 100 years old!). However, these fares often cost more than if you used excursion fares, also referred to as Supersaver, MaxSaver, and UltraSaver fares, where the discount may be 50 percent or more. Often "limited time only" promotional fares offer even more savings (up to 80 percent) at certain times when airlines are looking to fill seats. There is no difference between the seating, service, or aircraft on a full-coach or economy ticket and an excursion/promotional fare ticket. However, there are usually only a certain number of these cut-price seats available on each flight, so it is important to book as early as possible. In fact, if you are going to use your senior discount with a Supersaver fare, you will most likely be required to make your reservations at least 30 days in advance.

SuperSaver and MaxSaver fares carry a number of important restrictions. There are usually hefty cancellations fees, ticket change fees, blackout periods, a 7 to 30 day cancellation requirement, a 24 hour payment requirement, round-trip purchase requirement, Saturday night stayover, and other conditions. Always ask about all applicable restrictions before purchasing your tickets. You need to decide whether these limitations and

inconveniences are worth the savings. If you are flexible
in your plans, they usually are.

There are four ways airlines are currently using to
attract mature travelers:

1. Clubs with discounts (frequent flyers)
2. Straight discounts.
3. Unlimited-mileage passes.
4. Coupon books.

The minimum age for discount senior fares is 50,
usually honored in conjunction with proof of membership in AARP. However, check with individual airlines
since some offer senior rates starting at age 60 or older.
Most programs allow a companion of any age, regardless
of sex or relationship to travel at the same reduced fare.

When choosing among the confusing, ever-
changing fares airlines offer, always ask for the lowest
current fare. Check local newspaper advertisements,
travel magazines, or one of the several excellent travel
newsletters for the latest promotional offers.

Let them know that you qualify for a senior discount, but be aware that you may get a better deal by
going with a special promotion or supersaver fare.
Sometimes your senior discount can cut these low
fares even lower. You may even get lucky and hit a
special promotional fare for seniors (these are usually
run during off-peak seasons). These fares are often
significantly lower than other fares and may be the
cheapest way to go.

Yearly passes and discount coupon books are
available for seniors who do a significant amount of
traveling. Before purchasing either of these options,

however, it is important to determine how many trips you're likely to be making over the next year. Coupon booklets can be purchased in four or eight-coupon sets, each coupon being good for a one-way domestic flight. Seven to fourteen day advance reservations are nearly always required.

Most coupons are good for all destinations that an airline flies within the continental United States. Travel to Alaska or Hawaii usually requires using two coupons. Currently Alaska, America West, TWA, Continental, Northwest, American, Delta, United and USAir offer senior coupon programs. Prices range from $400 to $600 for books of four one-way coupons, and from $750 to $1000 for books of eight one-way coupons. Coupons are valid for one year from the purchase date and earn frequent flyer credit. However, if you don't think you'll be doing enough flying with a single airline to justify the cash outlay, you may be better off with regular senior citizen discounts or searching out excursion fares. The same rule for frequent flying applies to buying a multi-use domestic or international "passport" or air pass from an airline.

Tip: Remember all airlines now require a picture I.D. when you check in. So be prepared to present a valid proof of age with photo and, if applicable, your club/airline membership card.

Airline Discounts

American Air Lines. 800-421-5600. Active American Traveler Club. American Airlines/American Eagle offers three senior citizen discount programs:

1. 10 percent Senior TrAAveler Discount if you are 62 or older. Discount is valid at all times and may also be applied to a companion ticket.
2. Senior TrAAvelers coupon books can be purchased by travelers 62 or older. Four one-way 2,000 mile coupons cost $596.
3. Special Discount for AARP members. Members receive a 10 percent discount off lowest-published round-trip fares, including promotional fares, for flights within the United States, the Caribbean, and Mexico.

Active American Travel Club: Register online for the chance to win a free trip to Maui. Must be 62 or older, $40 annual fee. Web site: www.aa-aatc.com.

Continental Airlines www.continental.com. Senior fares: 800-441-1135. If you are 62 or over, you are eligible for a 10 percent discount on all fares on Continental. Now that you have the freedom to travel, you can also save when you join Continental's Freedom Flight Club. This special airfare program, created exclusively for travelers age 62 and over allows you to save 15 to 20% on Continental Airlines and Continental Express flights on any fare anywhere you want to travel. The cost is $579 for four one-way coupons. Coupons are valid for travel to all destinations in the mainland United States, Alaska, or Hawaii (two coupons required for Alaska and Hawaii).

TWA www.twa.com. 800-221-2000. Senior Travel Pak: If you are 62 or older, TWA's Senior Travel Pak contains four coupons, each redeemable for one way travel within the Continental U.S., priced at $548 per pak.

Delta Airlines www.delta-air.com. 800-221-1212. Delta Airlines offers a 10 percent senior citizen discount for seniors 65 or over and a traveling companion of any age on the lowest available fares. This does not apply to Delta Express flights. Their "Young at Heart" discount plan includes coupon booklets of four for $596, each coupon being good for one-way reserved seat travel to all U.S. cities including Hawaii, Alaska, and San Juan. Booklets are valid for one year from the date of purchase. **Note:** there are no discounts available online at the Delta site. You must ask when you are booking the flight about the discounts.

Northwest Airlines www.nwa.com. 800-692-6961. Offers three discount programs for senior travelers 62 or over.
1. "World Horizons" program. 10 percent senior citizen discount off most domestic fares for travelers 62 or over. No membership fee and all flights earn frequent-flyer credit.
2. "NorthBest Senior Travel Coupons." Travelers 62 or over can purchase four or eight one-way discount coupon booklets for flights in the continental United States and Canada (Alaska or Hawaii flights require two coupons). Guest certificates entitle accompanying companion to reduced fares. Four-coupon book costs $560. 14-day advance purchase is required.

3. "WorldPerks Senior." Members get a free trip every 20,000 miles and additional benefits and discounts including newsletter, hotel, car rental, cruise discounts, and reduced fee in WorldClub membership.

You can also earn up to 14,500 World Perk Miles by switching to Sprint when you sign up. Contact your travel agent or call Northwest Airlines Reservations at 800-225-2525 to enroll.

United Airlines www.silverwingplus.com. 800-241-6522. Travelers 55 or over receive 10 percent off coach/economy round-trip fares. Travelers 55 or over can join United's "Silver Wings Plus Travel Club." Members are entitled to 10 to 50 percent discounts on Clarion Hotels, Westin Hotels and Resorts, Hyatt Hotels and Resorts, Comfort Inns, and Quality Inns. Other benefits include discounts on Hertz, Alamo, and Dollar rental cars, a $25 discount certificate, and a quarterly travel magazine. Life membership is $225. A two-year membership is $75.

US Air www.usair.com. 800-428-4322. Senior travelers who are 62 years of age or older have two convenient ways to save when flying on US Airways. First, the Senior Saver Program offers a 10 percent discount on most fares, including the lowest discounted ones. When purchasing an airline ticket, if you are 62 years of age or older, tell the US Airways Reservations Sales Representative or your travel consultant that you are a senior, and begin saving. To book senior discounts on www.usairways.com, please type "Senior" in the "Special Instructions" text field when you "Buy" your reservations. (This option is not available when you "Express Buy" or "Hold.") Travel applies within the United States and between the United States and Canada. One companion of any age traveling with you will also receive the 10 percent discount when using the same fare and fare rules. You may need to provide proof of age when checking in at the airport.

Second, US Airways Golden Opportunities Coupon Books help seniors stretch travel dollars when flying to any US Airways destination in the U.S., Canada, Mexico, Puerto Rico or the U.S. Virgin Islands. These booklets include four one-way coupons, and are available for purchase at $579 U.S. or $861 Canadian. Plus, a single one-way coupon can be used for a roundtrip journey between any two Florida cities. And, Coupon-Book holders may use coupons for grandchildren between the ages of 2 and 11 who travel with them. Up to two grandchildren are permitted per coupon book holder.

Coupon books are valid for one year from the issue date. Reservations must be made at least 14 days prior to each departure. Passengers may travel standby anytime after tickets are issued. US Airways Dividend Miles program members receive mileage credits. Travel on a coupon is permitted any day of the week. Travel must originate in the country of coupon book purchase.

For more information about Senior Saver Fares, Golden Opportunities Coupon Books, and other senior programs, call US Airways at 800-428-4322.

U.S. Regional Airlines

Alaska Airlines www.alaskaair.com. 800-ALASKAAIR (1-800-252-7522). If you are 62 or over, Alaska Airlines offers a 10 percent senior citizen discount on any published fare. A companion of any age traveling with you receives the same discount. Senior discount coupon books are available for travel within the United States and Canada. Four one-way coupons cost $472 and eight one-way coupons cost $790. Travel to Alaska requires using two coupons each direction.

Aloha Airlines. 800-367-5250. If you're flying within the Hawaiian Islands, Aloha Airlines offers 10 percent off one-way fares for those over 60.

America West www.americawest.com. 800-235-9222. Senior fares give travelers 62 or over discounts between 10 and 50 percent off normal coach fares depending on route taken. America West also offer "Senior Saver Packs," discount booklets of four one-way coupons ($548). Coupons are valid to all U.S. cities except Hawaii. Coupon booklets are good for one year. **Note:** America West no longer flies to Japan or Hawaii.

Hawaiian Air www.hawaiinair.com. 800-367-5320. This inter-island airline offer discounts between 7–9% if you are 60 or over.

Midwest Express/Skyway Airlines www.midwest express.com. 800-452-2022. A 10% discount on all fares is offered for seniors over 62.

Southwest Airlines www.southwestairlines.com. 800-435-9792. Travelers 65 and over receive special senior discounts on flights between 9 A.M.–3 P.M., Monday–Thursday and all day Saturday. There is also a coupon program good for flights to all Southwest destinations. Fares range from $19–$99. Coupons are valid every day with no advance purchase required. Reservations are necessary. **Note:** All senior fare tickets are fully refundable. Web site for senior plans: www. iflyswa.com/info/seniors.htm.

Canadian Airlines

The following airlines in Canada offer 10 to 50 percent discounts for senior citizens 62 and over with proof of age. Companions traveling on the same itinerary also receive the discount. Ask whether discounts apply during the time you plan to travel.

Air Canada. 888-247-2262.

Canadian Airlines International. 800-426-7000.

European Airlines

Alitalia www.alitaliausa.com. 800-223-5730. If you are 62 or over and a member of United Airlines "Silver Wings Plus Travel Club," Alitalia offers you a 10 percent discount on certain flights. Alitalia also allows one person traveling with you to get the same fare.

British Airways. 800-247-9297. Offers the Privileged Traveller Program (60 or over), which entitles members to a 10 percent senior discount on all air fares. There are no penalties for cancellations or changed itineraries (before the day prior to departure) and no blackout periods. Members also receive a 10 percent discount on all Venice Simplon Orient Express departures, and British Airway Holiday Tours.

El Al www.elal.com. 800-223-6700 or 212-768-9200 in N.Y. If you are 60 or over, you are eligible for a 15 percent discount on El Al flights.

KLM Royal Dutch Airlines www.klm.com. 800-447-4747. If you are 65 or over and a member of United Airlines "Silver Wings Plus Travel Club," KLM Airlines offers you a 10 percent discount on any flight. Also, KLM lowers its fares in the off-season for those 65 or over on flights to many cities in the Netherlands.

Lufthansa. 800-645-3880. If you are 62 or over, Lufthansa offers 10 percent discounts on their fares.

TAPAir Portugal www.tap-airportugal.pt. 212-969-5775. Offers small senior discounts for those over 60 (and their companions) traveling during off-peak times.

Scandanavian Airlines (SAS) www.flysas.com. 800-437-5804. Travelers 65 or over receive a discount on some flights within Sweden.

Most major airline travel clubs (including American, Continental, Northwest, TWA, United and

USAir) offer special savings for mature adults. There is an initiation fee ranging between $50 and $150.

Take a Cruise for Less

How do you like the idea of a traveling resort? You unpack once and the rest of your transportation plans are taken care of. A recent survey of American travelers found that almost half of all cruise passengers are over 50. Cruise travel opportunities are nearly endless: Caribbean, Mediterranean, Alaska, South Pacific, the Orient, Hawaii, the Mexican Riviera, Baja California, South America, New England, Eastern Canada, Scandinavia, British Isles, the Mississippi and other rivers, through England, the wine country of France, and the Rivers of Germany. You can cruise just about anywhere there's enough water for a ship.

Cruises offer some of the best travel bargains available. If you book your trip far in advance (a year or more) or very close to the date of sailing you can save a bundle, 50% or more off the list price. You can also put yourself on "standby" for an upcoming cruise. Check the travel section of your newspaper for advertisements for last-minute cruise travel.

Agencies that specialize in last-minute travel can offer deep discounts. Although they are called "last-minute," several of them will book passengers in advance knowing these huge ships usually have space available. Last Minute Travel Agencies:

Encore Short Notice www.emitravel.com. 800-638-8976. Save up to 50% at Encore on certain packages.

Moment's Notice www.moments-notice.com. 213-486-0505.

Vacations To Go www.vacationstogo.com. 800-338-4962.

Last Minute Travel Club. 416-449-5400 or 877-970-3500.

You can also save if you book through a cruise discounter. In this case, you should be knowledgeable about individual cruise ships, itineraries, cabin locations, etc. A listing of cruise specials called "World of Cruising" is offered free by Cruise Line, Inc., a Miami based discount cruise and information center. For information call 800-777-0707.

When planning your cruise, ask for special cruise values during "shoulder" (between high and low season) and "off" seasons. The cruise is the same, but the price is less if you can travel during times when the demand is lower.

Cruise costs vary according to destination. Prices for a cruise include nearly everything: stateroom, lavish meals, entertainment, pool facilities, gymnasium, social programs, some shore tours and other activities. Compare the prices with the prices you are quoted by your travel agent. Your travel agent can also reserve dinner seating, arrange connecting air and ground transportation, suggest and book pre- and post-cruise tours, and advise on passport and visa requirements.

Be sure to research your cruise before you go. Get real-life travel stories and cruise reviews from seniors like yourself. Also try visiting the web site www. cruiseopinion.com.

Cruises for Seniors

Looking for a cruise specifically designed for seniors? Try these outfits:

Premier Cruise Lines www.thebigredboat.com, www.premiercruises.com. 800-373-2654. E-mail: premier@sunshine1.com. Discounts vary depending on the type of cruise you take and the time of year you sail. I recommend contacting a travel agent for rates and additional information. Or you may call Premier's reservation sales department at 800-990-7770. They are available until 8:00 P.M. on weeknights and 5:00 P.M. on weekends.

Note: This is Walt Disney World's official cruise line. The company offers a 10 percent discount to travelers 59 or over. Cruise packages generally include round trip air fare, a three or four night cruise to the Bahamas out of Port Canaveral, Florida, a three or four night stay in a hotel near Disney World, (anybody else who shares your cabin gets the 10 percent discount), plus free admission to Disney's Magic Kingdom, Spaceport USA, Epcot Center, Disney-MGM Studios Theme Park and a rental car with unlimited mileage.

Sea Escape Cruise Lines www.seaescape.com. 800-327-7400; in Florida: 800-432-0900. This cruise line offers one-day cruises with special discounts for mature travelers over 55 years. Cruise ships leave from Port Canaveral, Fort Lauderdale, St. Petersburg,

Miami, and Tampa. The best discounts are in the early summer months between April and June. Sea Escape offers seniors an average of $15 off regular prices.

Cruise One www.cruiseone.com. 800-327-SHIP; in Florida: 305-739-7447. This cruise line specializes in trips to the Far East, Alaska, Europe, Caribbean, Mexico, South Pacific, Panama Canal, and South America with special reduced rates. Senior travelers receive additional savings.

Special Interest Cruises

One of the most interesting concepts in cruises is the "educational" or "special interest" cruise. These cruises offer high-I.Q. itineraries for people who like the convenience of cruising, but want a vacation with more mental stimulation than shipboard bingo, shopping, and shore excursions. These innovative travel programs are offered by cruise lines, museums, university alumni associations, special interest magazines and other groups. They feature lecturers, expedition leaders and naturalists who are experts in their fields of interest. Some programs are on expedition ships especially designed to reach remote destinations.

Nonprofit groups and cruise companies that sponsor "special interest" cruises:

American Museum of Natural History www.amnh.org. 800-462-8687.

National Audubon Society www.audobon.org. 212-979-3000.

Smithsonian National Associate Program www.si.edu. 202-786-3280.

Stanford Alumni Association www.stanfordalumini. org. 605-723-2300.

World Wildlife Fund Expeditions www.world widelife.org. 888-WWF-TOUR (993-8687).

Classical Cruises. 800-252-7745.

Clipper Cruises. www.clippercruise.com. 800-325-0010. E-mail: smallship@aol.com.

Galapagos Cruises www.classicalcruises.com. 800-527-2500.

Renaissance Cruises www.renaissancecruises.com. 800-525-5350.

Salen Lindblad Cruising www.800-800-cruise.com.

Society Expiditions www.societyexpeditions.com. 800-548-8669.

Swan Hellenic Cruises www.swan-hellenic.co.uk. 877-219-4239.

World Explorer Cruises www.wecruise.com. 800-854-3835.

Most groups say their typical passengers are seasoned travelers around age 55. Although these types of trips are generally not a bargain, they do offer a stimulating, intellectual atmosphere not usually found aboard typical cruise ships.

Bus and Railroad Excursions

If you prefer to travel by bus or train, consider the following:

Greyhound Lines, Inc. www.greyhound.com. P.O. Box 660362, Dallas, TX 75266-0362. 800-229-9424 or 800-752-4841 (for passengers with disabilities).

Greyhound has introduced its new Seniors Club, available to all passengers age 62 and older. With the Seniors Club Card, members are eligible for the following:

- 10% off any unrestricted Greyhound passenger fare
- 10% off of food items at Greyhound owned and operated restaurants
- 10% off Greyhound Charter Services
- 25% off Greyhound Package Express shipments (prepaid personal shipments only)

Members are able to take advantage of the savings immediately and continue to enjoy the benefits for an entire year. The cost of the Greyhound Senior's Club is only $5.00, and applications are available at the Greyhound terminals nationwide. Seniors that are not members of the Senior's club may still request a 5% discount at a terminal counter on unrestricted passenger fares. Appropriate ID is required.

Gray Line Tours www.grayline.com. 303-433-9800. E-mail: info@grayline.com. Gray Line Tours motor coach company operates in cities throughout the United States. It offers 10 percent off half-day and full-day sightseeing tours at participating locations throughout the United States, Canada and Mexico for members of AARP and other senior organizations. To obtain the discount, purchase tour tickets directly from Gray Line and show a valid AARP Membership card. AARP discounts are not available at the following Gray Line locations: Alaska, Banff, Alberta, Chicago, Flagstaff, Jackson Hole, WY, Las Vegas, NV, Savannah, GA, Seattle/Tacoma, WA, and Victoria British Columbia; Whitehouse, Yukon territory and Yellowstone, MT.

For a list of National Tour Association member companies or information about specific motor coach tours contact: National Tour Association, Inc., North American Headquarters, 546 East Main St, Lexington, KY 40508-2300, or call 800-682-8886.

Travelers interested in motor coach tours can also check with their local Automobile Club Association office for information.

Senior citizens 62 and over and handicapped mature travelers are entitled to a 15 percent discount on Amtrak by presenting appropriate identification. The discounts are not restricted on holidays. Discounts do not apply to first class accommodations. There are no requirements to buy closed-end round-trip tickets. The senior discounts apply to any regular one-way fare of $50 or more, but buying a round-trip ticket is the most economical way to go. There is no charge or stopovers on one-way tickets, but you must report a stopover when making ticket reservations.

Amtrak operates trains and Metroliners that have reserved seating: coach and club car (first class) seats are available on Metroliners, which service most major Atlantic Coast cities and major metropolitan destinations throughout the United States. Sleeping cars are available between long distances. Snack bars are provided on most trains, and on overnight travel there are dining cars serving meals during the day and evening. For information contact: 800-USRAIL or 800-321-8684. Web site: www.amtrak.com.

Via Rail www.viarail.ca. 20 King Street West, Floor 5, Toronto, Ontario M5II 1 C4, Canada. 514-871-6349. Spending a night on board? VIA offers you Sleeper first class, with your own private bedroom or semi-private section, a comfortable bed, and access to a shower. In a sleeping car, the train is more like a cozy hotel! Other conveniences will help make your trip more enjoyable. For example, people with restricted mobility can board the train ahead of others.

If you are over 60, VIA offers you a 10% discount. There's one condition: if you don't look old enough, a member of their personnel might ask for proof of age. If you are planning to travel for several days during a 30-day period, find out about the Canrailpass. As a senior, you'll be entitled to buy a pass at an even lower price.

Tip: The rest room is in the same car, at the end of the wide aisle. On most long haul trips, you can enjoy a cup of coffee or tea in the Skyline. Several other trains have a restaurant car, where their chef prepares delicious meals with which you can enjoy a fine wine.

Renting a Car

The key to obtaining the best rate when renting a car is to reserve one in advance. When you call about rates or reservations, always have available a valid driver's license, a major credit card, your senior organization's ID number and you own membership card for reference. Never rent a car without getting a discount or a special promotional rate. Always ask for the lowest rate available at that time.

Most major car rental companies have toll-free reservation offices for reserving a car most anywhere in the world. Below are car rental agencies (and their web sites) that offer special senior rates or discounts:

Alamo www.goalamo.com. 800-GO-ALAMO. Alamo gives up to 20% discounts on car rentals to senior drivers and members of Classic Travel Club run by Travelodge, Days Inns' September Days Club, AARP, and United Silver Wings. Ask about the "Golden Wheels" program.

Avis www.avis.com. 800-331-1800. Avis offers special car rental discounts of 5 to 10 percent to senior citizens and members of Mature Outlook, AARP and CARP.

Budget/Sears Rent-A-Car budget.com. 800-527-0700. Offers daily rental discounts to members of AARP, Mature Outlook, Days Inns' September Days Club, and other senior organizations. Discounts vary depending on day or time of year.

Dollar <u>dollarcar.com</u>. 800-654-3131. Dollar offers discounts to senior citizens 60 and over and members of AARP.

Hertz <u>www.hertz.com</u>. 800-654-2200. Hertz offers 10 to 15% discounts to members of United Airlines' Silver Wings Plus Club, Days Inns' September Days Club, AARP, Y.E.S., and Mature Outlook.

National <u>www.nationalcar.com</u>. 800-CAR-RENT. National offers special discounts of 5 to 30% to members of Northwest Airlines' World Horizons Program, AARP, and Mature Outlook.

Thrifty Rent-A-Car <u>www.thrifty.com</u>. 800-367-2277. Members of Northwest Airlines' World Horizons Program, AARP, CARP, Mature Outlook, and Days Inns' September Days Club are entitled to 10 percent senior discounts on car rentals worldwide. Seniors must be 55 years of age or older.

Group Tour Programs

Tour programs come in many varieties from complete, door to door escorted excursions with everything planned and included, to highly individual programs where you are mostly on your own. Twenty-five years ago the idea of "taking a tour" meant taking a couple of weeks and covering several cities. Some companies still offer these breathless, whirlwind tours, but most are planned for a more relaxing, quality experience and are generally much less frantic. Your travel agent should recommend member tour operators of the National Tour Association (NTA), an organization requiring financial and performance standards of its members.

A tour package generally covers everything, including most meals, transportation, escorts, sightseeing, group parties, etc. You are required to pay for the full tour in advance. Less-structured tours allow for individual travel activities, with airfare, hotel, airport transfers, and some meals, admissions, etc. included in the package. Since professional tour operators deal in large volume bookings at lower rates, the cost for a package tour is usually lower than if you were to pay for the elements separately.

To help you decide on a tour, make a list of your travel likes, dislikes, preferences, etc. Study brochure descriptions, which usually include details of daily itineraries and organized activities. This will aid you in choosing a tour that is right for you, either one that is strictly scheduled, loosely scheduled with lots of free time, or one somewhere in between. Senior citizen discounts offered by tour operators vary by company, season, and other factors. As with all travel arrangements, ask your travel agent if there is a senior citizen discount for the tour you will be taking.

Some companies that focus their tour programs on mature travelers are:

Arthur Frommers Budget Tours www.frommers.com. Frommer's Travel Guides, 1633 Broadway New York, NY 10019. "Special travelers are those whom the travel industry sometimes regards as 'problems'— elderly singles, teenagers, the disabled, intellectuals, families with very, very small children, single-minded 'special interest' vacationers, persons traveling to attend a funeral, unaccompanied women, unaccompanied men, and more. For each such group, I attempt not simply to supply general advice, but the specific names, addresses and numbers of companies eager to serve them, travel firms that regard other companies' 'problem passengers' as their 'opportunities'"

Pleasant Hawaiian Holidays www.pleasant.net. 2404 Townsgate Road, Westlake Village, CA 91361. 800-242-9244. This company offers trips for those 60 and over to the Hawaiian Islands. Trips include flights, lodging (hotel or condo), side trips to other islands, breakfast, a rental car, transfers, counselors, a lei, and a memory album. There is a complimentary upgrade for seniors (when available) on room and car rentals.

Autumn Years Tours. 21 E. 26th St., New York, NY 10010. 800-854-0103; 212-689-8977. This British travel agency offers escorted motor coach tours to those over 55. Most of the excursions are in Europe: England, Belgium, Holland, Germany, Austria, Switzerland, France, and Italy. Tour members are escorted by British tour directors.

Tips for Traveling Abroad
Passports
Passports are required for entry into most foreign countries. Make sure yours is up to date; passports issued prior to 1982 are good for 8 years; passports issued after 1983 are good for 10 years. To apply for a

passport contact your federal government building information center or the Passport Agency. Also, check with your local U.S. post office or local courthouse.

Apply for a passport two to three months prior to a planned trip, as it can take up to six weeks to process your application. You will need two photographs—one in color and one in black and white-to get your passport.

Currency

Get U.S. denomination travelers' checks through your bank. Traveler's checks are safer than cash, and if you don't use there, they can be used like money when you get home. Also, you won't have to pay an exchange fee to convert them back, like you do with foreign currency. Exchange most of your currency after you arrive since exchange rates are usually better in banks abroad. If you wish to exchange tour dollars into foreign currencies before you leave, just exchange enough for incidentals like tips and taxis. Cash personal checks only as you need them. Again this will avoid having to exchange extra foreign currency back into dollars for a fee.

Tip: In order to avoid carrying too much cash, bring an ATM (Automatic Teller Machine) card with you that is on a international world-wide system. Nearly every 'Westenized" country in the world has ATM machines on practically every corner. It's a simple way to get as much cash as you need in the currency you need. For example, Spain has more ATMs than any country in the world. They are everywhere, from the smallest villages to large cities.

Vaccinations

In some areas of the world, particularly the tropics, you need certain vaccinations to protect your health. Ask your travel agent or call your state or local health department about required inoculations or vaccinations. Some medications and vaccinations must be taken two to four weeks in advance of travel, so check far enough ahead to be safe.

The Center for Disease Control www.cdc.gov in Atlanta has a 24-hour hotline with international health requirements and health recommendations for foreign travelers. Call 800-311-3435 or 877-FYI-TRIP.

Visas

Similar to passports, visas are international identification cards. Ask your travel agent which countries require visas, or call the embassies of the countries you plan to visit. Visas are issued through the particular country's embassy in Washington, D.C., or the nearest consular office.

Warning: There are some countries for which travel advisories are issued by the State Department because of uncertain or unsafe conditions for American travelers. The State Department maintains an Advisory Hotline, 202-647-5225, which you can call for updated information. Also, the Sunday travel section of the newspaper of a large city will also carry briefs about which countries are not recommended for current travel.

Customs

You can bring up to $400 worth of new merchandise into the United States from abroad without paying taxes on it. The next $1,000 worth of goods is generally taxed at a 10 percent rate. The U.S. Customs Service publishes a free booklet "Know Before You Go," explaining all the customs procedures. For a copy write: Department of the Treasury, U.S., Customs Service, 1300 Pennsylvania Avenue NW Room 54D, Washington, DC 20229.

The U.S. State Department has a brochure designed to alert Americans to potential risks of foreign travel and to raise security awareness. Topics include: how to contact American consulates or embassies in emergencies; how to obtain current travel advisories on hot spots around the world; and tips on medical matters, travel insurance and visas. For a free copy write for "What You Should Know Before You Go," Americans Abroad, Pueblo, CO 81009.

Tip: Look up the Federal Consumer Information Center web site at www.pueblo.gsa.gov. There are hundreds of free booklets on dozens of subjects published by this department of the government. Click on "Travel" and find the booklets that are of most interest to you. You can also write them at Pueblo, CO 81002 for a complete current catalog.

Traveling with the Grandkids

If you have grandchildren, traveling with them can be inexpensive, educational and can strengthen the bonds between you and your grandchildren. Many folks feel children between 7 and 13 travel best. As for saving money, airlines often offer discounts for children under 12 (as well as special companion fares) and most hotels allow them to stay in the same room with their grandparents at no extra charge. Cruise lines sometimes offer last-minute specials when they are under booked, allowing kids to travel completely free. Travel with one of the groups below and not only see the world, but improve relationships and communication between generations.

El Al's Generation to Generation Tours. 800-223-6700 or 212-768-9200. EL AL, the Israeli national airline, offers vacation opportunities for grandparents and grandchildren to Israel. Trips are planned so that visits to such places as Jerusalem, Tel Aviv, Masada, and the Dead Sea include special activities for both generations.

GrandTravel www.grandtravel.com. 9107 Grand Avenue, Franklin Park, IL 60131. 800-247-7651. This organization arranges tours for grandparents and grandchildren. GrandTravel's series of itineraries are scheduled for normal school breaks. They offer 15 tours, including travel to the western states and national parks, Washington, D.C., Alaska, Hawaii, an American Indian country tour, New England, the Soviet Union, Galapagos Islands, China and Japan, Africa, Scandinavia, Holland, England and Scotland, and New Zealand. Tours are developed by educators, psychologists, and leisure counselors and are structured to encompass both informational and recreational aspects. Trips focus on strengthening the bonds between the grandparent and grandchild, but there is plenty of time for everyone to be with people their own age.

Mayflower Tours.1225 Warren Avenue, PO Box 490, Downers Grove, IL 60515. 800-323-7604. Mayflower Tours offers special programs for senior citizens but does not have an age limit. Some senior travelers bring their grandchildren along on the tours. The minimum age for a child traveling on a Mayflower Tour is six years old.

Saga Holidays www.sagaholiday.com. Saga International Holidays, Ltd., 222 Berkley St, Boston, MA 02116. 877-265-6862. Saga offers special tours for folks over 60 traveling with children between 6 and 16. Trips to scenic areas and places of interest in the Northwest, American Southwest, the California Coast and national parks are scheduled during regular school breaks.

Vistatours www.vistatours.com. 1923 N. Carson Street, Suite 105, Carson City, NV 139701. 800-248-4782; 702-882-2100. Vistatours offers a special tour series for grandparents and grandchildren. The tour schedules time for adults to be together with other adults at the same time the children are with other children. Grandparents and grandchildren also participate in activities together, giving the two generations the opportunity to share their traveling experiences.

Adventure Travel

If you have a spirited sense of adventure and lots of energy, consider traveling with one of these groups that specialize in challenging, exciting travel experiences.

American Wilderness Experience www.gorptravel. com (a member of GORP Travel). PO Box 1486,

Boulder, CO 80306. 877-440-GORP. E-mail: info@gorp-travel.com. American Wilderness Experience offers mature adults discounts on backcountry travel. Trips include a Bridger-Teton backcountry horseback trip in Wyoming, Sangre de Cristo Mountains horseback trip in Colorado, Mountain Sports Week Adventure in Colorado, a Colorado Surf and Turf Combo in Colorado, and an Alaska Wildlands Senior Safari Tour. In order to be eligible for the senior discounts you must be 65.

Outward Bound USA www.outwardbound.org. 800-243-8520. Locations include North Carolina and Colorado. The Outward Bound organization is well known for its wilderness-survival courses that are aimed to help youngsters and young adults. Mature adults can also discover new ways to go beyond their limitations through Outward Bound's shorter courses designed specifically for adults over 50. Some of the courses have a special goal of easing the transition from career to retirement.

Be prepared to live in a tent, sleep in sleeping bags, and cook your own food. Good health is a requirement to participate. Adventures include: courses canoeing in the Florida Everglades, canoeing in the lake country of Minnesota, sailing in the Florida Keys, river rafting, desert backpacking or rock climbing on the West Coast, or white-river rafting or hiking in North Carolina.

American Youth Hostels www.hiayh.org. Dept. 855, PO Box 37613, Washington, D.C. 20013-7613. 202-783-6161. E-mail: hiayhserv@hiayh.org. This group coordinates more than 5,000 hostels in over 70 countries. The most relaxed and adventurous of mature singles stay in youth hostels both here and abroad, now that the international youth-hostel organization has removed all maximum age restrictions on the right to use their facilities. Particularly in the fall and winter months, when young people are in school, the predominant clientele of many youth hostels is today middle-aged and elderly! But even when one shares these multi-bedded rooms or dorms with young people, one pays an inexpensive charge, without a supplement. And one stays in a lively setting of international conversations and encounters.

Membership is $20 a year, but if you are 55, you only pay $10. AYH offers low-cost adventure trips for persons over 50 in its World Adventure trip program. Each trip is limited to 10 persons including a trip leader. You can tour all over the world by van, minibus, train, or bicycle. Some of their trips include: traveling by van to European cities; cycling in New England in the fall; a trip to the mountains, glaciers, and lakes of Alaska; five weeks by train and ferry through Europe; and hiking in the San Francisco Bay area.

Adventure Women www.adventurewomen.com. 15033 Kelly Canyon Road, Bozeman, MT 59715. 800-804-8686 (United States) or 406-587-3883 (Montana and outside United States). Exclusively for active women over 30, destinations include Timbuktu, the Amazon River, Alaska, the Sonoran Desert and Southern France.

World Wide Fishing www.worldwidefishing.com. PO Box 9076, Ketchikan, Arkansas 99901. 800-272-7291. Charter and sightseeing/fishing expeditions.

Africa Guide www.africaguide.com. Detailed information on traveling in 51 countries in Africa.

Eldertreks www.eldertreks.com. 800-741-7956. World's first travel company dedicated exclusively to people over 50. The group explores the culture and nature of a destination while traveling sensitively in small groups of 16 or less people. All trips involve walking and some include hiking in rainforests, deserts or mountain environments.

Pedal Power: Bike Trails

If you are a serious biker, you may want to consider taking a trip along the 4,250 miles of the America trail. This trail begins in Astoria, Oregon and goes to Yorktown, Virginia, winding its way across the country through small American towns. Campgrounds and inexpensive bike inns are situated along the way.

There are also several excellent companies that do nothing but plan biking tours, walking/hiking tours and other types of adventure travel. These companies offer trips all over the world for all levels of biking enthusiasts. Trips range from combination hiking/biking/backpacking vacations in Hawaii to luxury trips with gourmet meals and accommodations in four-star French chateaux and English castles. Check with your travel agent for information and brochures. Or check the listings in the back of some of the dozens of very interesting and informative travel magazines available at your local bookstore or magazine stand. Many of these companies advertise in the directories of these magazines.

U.S. National Park System and Recreational Areas

Our national park system includes some of the most breathtaking, magnificent areas on this planet. These areas are maintained and preserved by the government for use by all people who wish to experience the depth of our precious natural resources and the richness of our cultural history. Travelers can enjoy educational, stimulating vacations visiting our national parks, national wildlife reserves, recreation areas, monuments, and historic sites.

Some of these sites include: craters, swamps, seashores, caves, trading posts, battlefields, ships, military parks, historic homes, sand dunes, waterfalls, cliff dwellings, volcanoes, and giant redwood forests.

Information on national parks, historic sites, and monuments in the areas you plan to visit can be obtained free of charge by writing the National Park Service www.nps.gov, 1849 C Street, NW, Washington, DC 20240. 202-208-6843.

Since observing wildlife is a recreational hobby shared by many mature adults, you may want to visit one of the 450 National Wildlife Refuges that comprise over 90 million acres of lands and waters. Write to: Division of National Refuges, U.S. Fish and Wildlife Service, Department of the Interior, Washington, DC

20240, for brochures and information. Or look up the web site: www.fws.gov.

There are 156 national forests that stretch from Alaska to Puerto Rico that offer exciting opportunities for outdoor adventure. For a copy of "National Forest Vacations," write: U.S. Department of Agriculture, Forest Service, Agriculture Building, 12th Street and Independence Avenue SW, P.O. Box 96090, Washington, DC 20090. Each regional office of the Forest Service has maps and literature about recreational facilities in the national forests.

For information write to Regional Forester, USDA Forest Service at an area office listed below:

Alaska Region, 709 W. 9th St., Room 213A, Juneau, Alaska. 907-747-4259.

Pacific Southwest Region, 1323 Club Drive, Vallejo, California 94592. 707-562-8737.

Eastern Region, 310 West Wisconsin Avenue, Milwaukee, Wisconsin 53203.

Rocky Mountain Region, PO Box 25127, Lakewood, Colorado 80225-0127. 303-275-5350.

Intermountain Region, Federal Building, 324 25th St., Ogden, Utah 84401.

Pacific Northwest Region, PO Box 3623 SW First Avenue, Portland, Oregon 97208-3623.

Southwest Region, 517 Gold Avenue SW, Albuquerque, New Mexico 87102.

Southern Region, 1720 Peachtree Avenue, Atlanta, Georgia 30367. 404-347-4177.

Visit the web site at www.fs.fed.us.

Some organizations offer wilderness trips in the national forests. Trips are organized with regard to differing levels of ability, with several designed with mature adults in mind. For information write:

The Wilderness Society www.wilderness.org. 1400 Eye Street, Washington, DC 20005. 202-833-2300.

New England Hiking Holidays. PO Box 1648, North Conway, New Hampshire 03860. 800-869-0949.

The Golden Passports

Golden Eagle Passport

This is an entrance pass to those national parks, monuments, historic sites, recreation areas, and national wildlife refuges that charge an entrance fee. The Golden Eagle Passport costs $50 and is valid for one year from any date of purchase. You may purchase a Golden Eagle Passport at any NPS entrance fee area or by mail. In 1999, President Clinton purchased a Golden Eagle Passport at Grand Tetons.

The Golden Eagle Passport does not cover or reduce use fees, such as fees for camping, swimming, parking, boat launching, or cave tours. It is valid for entrance fees only. To purchase by mail, send a $50 check or money order (do not send cash) to: National Park

Service, 1100 Ohio Drive, SW Room 138, Washington, DC 20242, Attention: Golden Eagle Passport

Golden Age Passport

This is a lifetime entrance pass for those 62 years or older. The Golden Age Passport has a one time processing charge of $10. You must purchase a Golden Age Passport in person. It is not available by mail or telephone. This can be done at any NPS facility that charges an entrance fee. At time of purchase, you must show proof of age (62 years or older) and be a citizen or permanent resident of the United States.

The Golden Age Passport admits the pass holder and any accompanying passengers in a private vehicle. Where entry is not by private vehicle, the passport admits the pass holder, spouse, children and parents.

The Golden Age Passport also provides a 50% discount on federal use fees charged for facilities and services such as fees for camping, swimming, parking, boat launching, or cave tours. It does not cover or reduce special recreation permit fees or fees charged by concessionaires.

Golden Access Passport

This is a free lifetime entrance pass for persons who are blind or permanently disabled. It is available to citizens or permanent residents of the United States, regardless of age, who have been determined to be blind or permanently disabled. You may obtain a Golden Access Passport at any entrance fee area by showing proof of medically determined disability and eligibility for receiving benefits under federal law.

The Golden Access Passport also provides a 50% discount on federal use fees charged for facilities and services such as fees for camping, swimming, parking, boat launching, or cave tours. It does not cover or reduce special recreation permit fees or fees charged by concessionaires.

CHAPTER 4

Your Finances, Retirement and Insurance Made Easy

Finances and financial security, how to live within our means, and finding safe ways to invest our money are all major concerns for mature adults. In our "earning years," making money is our primary concern. As we approach retirement, keeping it becomes our main focus.

Retirement plans abound. There are seemingly endless numbers of investment firms, brokers, and counselors who would like to help you invest your money for retirement (which, of course, generates fees and commissions for them). Although there are many different types of plans available, I am going to show you how to get the best free and low-cost retirement savings investment advice, as well as how to find special savings available only to mature adults. I will also examine both how to obtain free health care

(when available) and how to find the most cost effective health care benefits and programs. As complex as
these issues seem, there are sources of information to
help us better understand them.

Free Stuff from the Bank

With banks and savings and loans in fierce competition for your funds, there has emerged a whole
new arena of privileges, perks, and special programs
for seniors. It is estimated that some 63 million
Americans age 50 and older hold approximately two
thirds of all bank the savings deposits, and approximately 80 percent of savings and loan deposits. It's
not difficult to understand why banks and S&Ls are
literally fighting for these funds. In most cases the
rate of investment return is virtually the same among
competing institutions, so they have come up with all
kinds of ways to entice us into saving with their particular organization. This translates into free benefits
for seniors including:
  • Free online banking
  • No or low-fee ATM-only or express checking
    account
  • Free checking accounts
  • Free safe deposit boxes
  • Free photocopying
  • Added percentage points on invested funds
  • Free checks
  • Free notary service
  • Free telephone and wire service transfers

- Free traveler's checks, cashier's checks and money orders
- Newsletters
- Waiver of service charges on bankcard membership
- Overdraft protection on checking accounts
- Seminars on tax-free investing, health, and fitness
- Free subscriptions to senior publications
- Travel discounts
- Membership in dining clubs
- Discounts on merchandise, entertainment, dental care, vitamins, eyewear, automobiles

These are some of the "extras" banks offer seniors and preferred customers to gain their business and lasting loyalty. Once you open an account or buy a CD, these banks are hoping you'll become interested in their trust services, home-equity loans, automobile loans, reverse mortgages, etc.

As in other industries, senior discounts and services are not always advertised or disclosed at first glance. You need to inquire as to what benefits you can receive. Make a list of the kinds of "extra" services you feel are important and present them to the bank officer responsible for new accounts. They may just offer you what you want. When deciding where to entrust your funds, compare requirements for maintaining minimum balances, service charges, and interest rates.

If you feel that your bank is not handling you or your business correctly you can turn to your State Banking Commissioner with your complaint. If you cannot resolve your problems with your bank (they are charging you too many fees, not approving loans, not offering basic services), then contact the Banking Commissioner's office and they will make an investigation. You can find the office in the government pages of your local phone directory.

If you are concerned about whether your deposited funds are insured (Treasury Bonds and certain notes are not), contact your nearest regional Federal Deposit Insurance Corporation office or the Division of Compliance and Consumer Affairs, FDIC, 550 17th St., NW, Washington, DC 20429. 800-934-3342. Web site: www.fdic.gov. They answer questions and take complaints regarding FDIC regulated institutions and your FDIC insured deposit. They also publish information on financial reports and the compliance of different institutions, free brochures and a quarterly newsletter.

Tax Relief

If you need information or help with your taxes, the IRS offers free publications on a large number of tax topics. In fact, there is an IRS publication that covers just about every item that appears on a Form 1040. Although these publications go into great detail, they are written simply and accurately. There is even a publication that contains a list of all the other free publications entitled: *Guide to Free Tax Services*. You can receive these publications by:

1. Calling the IRS's toll-free number 800-424-FORM;
2. Going to your local IRS office, post office, bank, or library and seeing whether their supply of bulletins includes what you are looking for; or

3. Writing the Forms Distribution Center for your state (the address is listed in the Form 1040 booklet).

The IRS also has a toll-free volunteer telephone tax assistance number for specific questions on filling out your forms. This service, called Volunteers In Tax Assistance (VITA), works best for those with simple returns. The number is: 800-TAX-1040. For more complex tax returns, a professional tax preparer, tax service, or accountant is recommended. Web site: www.irs.gov.

Copies of most IRS forms and help on how to fill them out is available online at www.irs.ustreas.gov.

The IRS also has a hotline service that allows you to speak to tax attorneys specializing in retirement and pension plan issues. Between 1:30 P.M. and 3:30 P.M., Monday thru Thursday you can call 202-622-6074 or 6076. This is a service of the Employee Plans Technical and Actuarial Division of the Internal Revenue Service.

Special Note: To read documents by the IRS, you will need a copy of Adobe Acrobat Reader on your computer. You can get a free copy of this software at www.adobe.com.

"Protecting Older Americans Against Over-payment of Income Taxes," is a free publication published by the Special Committee on Aging. The purpose of this publication is to ensure that older Americans understand and claim all the legal deductions they are entitled to. Write for it at: Special Committee on Aging, U.S. Senate, SDG 30, Washington DC 40410. 202-224-5364. Or you can look them up at www.senate.gov/committee/aging.html.

In addition, the AARP www.aarp.com has over 8,000 Tax-Aide service sites manned by volunteer tax counselors who help low- and moderate-income tax-payers over 60 with filing their income tax returns. For information call your local AARP chapter or check their web site.

H&R Block www.hrblock.com has downloadable software that you can check to make sure everything is in the right place on your tax return.

CCH Internet Tax Research Network www.cch.com provides helpful hints about preparing for tax season and filing your individual return.

The search engine YAHOO! has a Tax Center www.yahoo.com/government/taxes that will help you find other tax help on the Internet. Their directory of links is comprehensive and should lead you to answers to your questions.

Retirement Recommendations

There are several sources of free and low cost information and advice on how to prepare for retirement. The Administration on Aging publishes booklets covering retirement topics including:

"Every Tenth American," describing the programs of the Administration on Aging;

"Are You Planning on Living the Rest of Your Life?" a do-it-yourself planner for people without pre-retirement counseling services provided by their jobs;

"You, the Law and Retirement," which explains when and why to see a lawyer;

"Consumer Guide for Older People," a wallet-size folder that outlines ways older folks can protect themselves against rip-offs, frauds, and swindlers.

To receive any of these booklets write: U.S. Department of Health and Human Services, Commission on Aging, 330 Independence Ave., SW, Washington, DC 20201. Or call 800-677-1116. Look them up online at: www.aoa.gov and www.hhs.gov.

Retirement Planning Associates www.retirement-planning.com. 818-781-7721. At what age can you afford to retire? RPA will help you decide.

Metlife offers a large variety of free brochures in a series that covers insurance, business, money, health and family issues. Call them at 800-638-5433 or check on their web site for the latest information: www.lifeadvice.com. The series is called "Life Advice." You can also write MetLife at One Madison Avenue, New York, NY 10010.

Financial Engines on the Web www.financial engines.com. Sign up and receive a free prospectus/outlook.

IDS Financial Services has a free booklet entitled "What Do I Want to Be . . . I Retire? Financial Planning for Retirement," which explains how much money you will need to retire and ways to minimize taxes, update your will and check your health insurance. It also lists groups that can help. They also publish a free 20-page guide, "Financial Planning: How It Works For You." For either publication write: IDS Consumer Affairs, IDS Financial Services, Inc., IDS Tower 10, Minneapolis, MN 55440.

Another source of information available through Commerce Clearing House is "On Your Retirement: Tax and Benefit Considerations." This booklet discusses Social Security and Medicare benefits, private pensions and annuities, IRAs, and tax breaks available to older Americans. Copies are $5, plus tax, handling and shipping. Write: Commerce Clearing House, Inc. 4025 W. Peterson Ave., Chicago, IL 60646 or call them toll-free at 800-248-3248.

John Hancock Financial Services www.jhancock. com will send you a free "Retirement Planning Guide" showing you how much money you'll need for a comfortable retirement. Write to: John Hancock Mutual Funds, 101 Huntington Avenue, Boston, MA 02199-7603. Call 800-695-7389.

The Arthritis's Foundation Planned Giving Committee www.arthritis.org organizes volunteer attorneys and financial planners who speak on such topics as estate, financial, and tax planning. These seminars and workshops are offered free to the general public. Contact your local chapter of the Arthritis Foundation for a copy of the calendar of programs in your area.

The AFL-CIO puts out a brochure called "Aging & The Community," which offers information on how to enjoy your retirement to its fullest. Write them for this free publication at: Department of Community Services, AFL-CIO, 815 16th St. NW, Washington, DC 20006.

The New England Mutual Life Insurance Company www.massmutual.com has prepared a free guide "How to Prepare for a Financially Secure Retirement." For a copy write: The New England, 501 Boylston St, Boston, MA 02117. Contact MassMutual at 800-743-5274.

Your financial planner, accountant, insurance agent, or securities broker should be able to advise you on your choices of investment vehicles for safeguarding your money and insuring income for you and your family's future. Mutual funds, stock funds, bond funds, CDs, money market funds, tax-free income funds, taxable-income funds, growth-income funds, fixed-income funds, IRAs, Keoghs, annuities, reverse mortgages, living trusts, 401 (k) plans, etc., are just some of the investment alternatives and opportunities available in today's complex financial marketplace.

If you want to make sure your financial advisor/ planner, money manager, stockbroker or sales representative has not had any legal problems or disciplinary actions brought against him, you can call the toll-free hotline run by the National Association of Securities Dealers, Regulation department. They have information on civil judgments, criminal judgments, indictments, arbitrations, disciplinary actions and other actions taken by securities regulators. Call them at 800-289-9999 or look them up online at www.nasdr.com.

You can also run a background check on investment brokers by calling the hotline of the North American Securities Administrators Association at 800-942-9022 or call 202-737-0900. They will tell you who to call in your state.

The Securities and Exchange Commission www.sec.gov will also do a full background check on any company that offers public stock or on any brokerage firm. In addition, they also publish several free publications on investing wisely and safely. Write them at the Securities and Exchange Commission, Office of Consumer Affairs, 450 Fifth St., NW, Washington, DC 20549. Tel: 202-942-4040, 800-SEC-0330 (publications line).

If you are looking for a financial advisor or planner contact The International Association for Financial Planning, Registry of Financial Planning Practitioners, 2 Concourse Parkway #800, Atlanta, GA 30328. 404-395-1605 or 888-806-7526.

You can also contact the National Association of Personal Financial Advisors (fee-only planners) 888-FEE-ONLY, 800-366-2632. They will send you a list of their members and questions you should ask any financial planner in an interview before becoming a client. A professional money manager must be registered with the SEC. The Freedom of Information Branch of the SEC, 202-272-7440, or your state securities commission can check their records for you.

The Institute of Certified Financial Planners www.icfp.org publishes several brochures including "How to Manage Your Financial Resources: Creating a Spending

Plan You Can Control," and "Selecting a Qualified Financial Planning Professional: Twelve Questions to Consider." Call them toll-free at 800-282-7526 (consumer assistance program). Or write them at: 10065 East Harvard Avenue Denver, CO 80231. 800-322-4237.

Financial Tip: Always get an independent second opinion, or investigate yourself before investing.

A professional insurance agent should be a C.L.U., meaning chartered life underwriter or C.P.C.U., chartered property/casualty underwriter. Your state insurance commission (the number is in the state government listing section of your phone book) can give you records of disbarment.

For preparing taxes and other financial services, a professional accountant should be a certified public accountant (C.P.A.), licensed by the state. The state board of accountancy (the number is among the state government listings in the phone book) will let you know if any disciplinary or licensing actions have been brought forth.

For advice on buying, selling, or investing in real estate, work with a real estate broker or sales agent who is licensed by the state. They should also be a member of the National Association of Realtors or the local board of Realtors. Your state real estate commission (again, the number is in the state government listings in the phone book) can alert you to any past problems. Unless you know your agent well, investigate and get independent advice before buying.

An interesting and free source of information on investing for retirement can be found in the columns and features of senior magazines and newspapers.

Most publications have a regular section on personal finance and/or money matters. A variety of questions pertaining to seniors are addressed in these pages. Their in-depth articles can help clarify and explain a lot of the confusion regarding money and investments. Local libraries and senior citizen centers subscribe to most of these publications. They are also distributed free in markets and some restaurants.

Where to Go for Answers on Medicare and Insurance

You will probably qualify for Medicare at age 50, but the program currently only covers little more than a third of actual medical costs. Chances are you will need either a medical supplement policy or an all-inclusive HMO or health insurance program to add to or replace Medicare. Medicare was never intended to be an all-inclusive health insurance program, and these supplemental policies offer coverage and benefits not covered by Medicare.

Trying to make sense of the several health coverage options that are available can be difficult and confusing; however, there are sources of information and education to help you understand these options.

The toll free Medicare Hotline, 800-638-6833, assists seniors in their questions and will refer them to local offices. They also publish and distribute free information booklets including: "Guide to Health Insurance for People with Medicare," "Medicare and Managed Car Plans," "Medicare Coverage of Kidney Dialysis and Kidney Transplant Services," "Manual De Medicare

(Spanish Edition)," "Medicare and Your Physician's Bill," "Medicare: Hospice Benefits," "Medicare: Coverage for Second Surgical Opinion," and "Medicare and Other Health Benefits." You can also write them at: Medicare Hotline, Health Care Financing Administration, 6325 Security Blvd., Baltimore, MD 21207 or check the information on their web site: www.hcfa.gov.

"A Consumer's Guide to Long-Term Care Insurance" and "Health Care and Finances: A Guide for Adult Children and Their Parents," are available through the Consumer Information Catalog www.pueblo.gsa.gov, Consumer Information Center-N, PO Box 100, Pueblo, CO 81009. 800-688-9889.

The Senior Citizens Health Insurance Counseling program (SCHIC) is a free service provided by The National Association of Life Underwriters www.nahu.org, which helps seniors evaluate their health care needs and educates them about fraudulent insurance schemes and solicitations. Active or retired insurance agents in more than twenty states participate in the program. For information write: The National Association of Life Underwriters, 2000 North 14th St., Suite 450, Arlington, VA 22201. 703-276-0220.

The Health Insurance Association of America www.hiaa.org, 555 135th St. NW, Washington DC 20004, 202-824-1600, has two excellent free pamphlets entitled: "The Consumer's Guide to Medicare Supplement Insurance" and "The Consumer's Guide to Long-Term Care Insurance."

The Health Insurance Counseling and Advocacy Program (HICAP) of the California Dept. of Aging and the Legal Services Trust Fund organizes free educational programs and seminars on Medicare and HMOs through its Medicare Advocacy Project (MAP). MAP is an independent, nonprofit organization not affiliated with Medicare or any insurance company or Health Maintenance Organization. Senior citizen clubs, community centers, hospitals, medical centers and related organizations can schedule one of their specialists for a presentation. Some of the topics covered include: "Nuts and Bolts of Medicare," "Who Pays for Skilled Nursing and Long-Term Care?," "Filling the Medicare Gaps," "What Supplemental Insurance Can Do," and "What You Should Know Before Joining an HMO." For information on their programs call 510-839-0393.

The Arthritis Foundation will send you a free booklet on choosing a health plan to cover all your needs. Write them at PO Box 7669, Atlanta, GA 30357.

A free *Consumer's Guide to Insurance* is available from the Life & Health Insurance Foundation for Education, a non-profit group. This guide should help you through the maze of terms and plans and how much you should pay. Call them toll-free at 888-543-3777 or visit their web site: www.life-line.org.

The General Accounting Office (GAO) www.gao.gov wants to make sure you understand all the ramifications of long-term care insurance and the problems that can result from not paying premiums through your later years. Their series of free reports can be requested by writing: U.S. General Accounting office, PO Box 6015, Gaithersburg, MD 20884.

Most hospitals and medical centers also sponsor their own free seminars on investment management needs, health care, and life insurance. These are usually coordinated through their senior or geriatric health departments and are advertised in local newspapers, senior publications, and mailings. Check with the hospitals in your area for a schedule of upcoming seminars.

In addition, some of the large federally qualified health plan organizations sponsor lectures and presentations throughout the year at various locations. Their schedules are usually advertised in local senior publications and magazines. Two examples are Secure Horizons www.securehorizons.com and Senior Plan FHP Health Care.

Senior newspapers and magazines, along with their recommendations on investment and money matters, offer a wealth of interesting and informative advice in all areas of health care and insurance. Nearly every publication has a regular feature or column answering readers' questions on these subjects. These "health" columnists and editors are specialists in their field and offer consumers sound advice and referrals for additional information. These publications also feature monthly calendar listings of dozens of free lectures, screenings, health fairs and expos, flu shot clinics, etc. By taking advantage of these free community services, you can save yourself a lot of money on what is generally routine, preventive health care that costs a lot more with a private practitioner.

Automobile Insurance

Some insurance companies offer discounts on automobile insurance rates for seniors, who incidentally have better driving records than other age groups. Most independent agents represent at least one company offering special senior rates. Examples of insurance companies that give "senior rates" for good drivers include: State Farm Insurance Company, Nationwide Insurance, Liberty Mutual Insurance Group, and Allstate Insurance Company. The AARP also has an automobile insurance program, and several of the national senior organizations offer insurance discounts with membership. Your automobile club may also offer special discounts to their senior members who drive. Check with the individual organizations for their benefits.

CHAPTER 5

You're Never Too Old to Learn

Education is a lifetime process. Now, for the first time in many of our lives, we can choose to learn about the things we really want to know. Our choices cover a wide spectrum, from regular graded classes and curriculum to special classes offered specifically for mature adults. As seniors, we make the decisions on where to study, what to study, and how much or how hard to study. Now is the time to expand your horizons and learn for your own personal enjoyment and growth.

Practically every institution in the United States and Canada welcomes older adults into its regular programs, with a large majority offering reduced tuition and fees. If you wish to take courses for credit towards earning a degree or diploma, you may do so. However, if you simply wish to add to your knowledge, most schools will allow you to audit or monitor their classes.

In addition to the education you are receiving, going back to school is a wonderful opportunity to increase your social contacts and make friends.

Younger students will benefit from working alongside a mature adult by gaining special insights from their life experiences and knowledge of the "real" world.

Learning Centers

A recent development in adult education that has gained popularity is the formation of adult learning centers offering a wide variety of short-term, practical, high-quality courses at reasonable fees. Most courses cost between $50 and $100 (except computer courses, which are usually under $200). Classes are taught by consultants, entrepreneurs, business owners, professionals, medical professionals, etc., who enjoy teaching adults in the community.

Programs center around topics such as finding new and unusual careers, improving relationships, self-improvement, real estate, hands-on computer literacy, money management, creative and career writing, hobbies, sports and recreation, living more spiritually, living healthier, entertaining, cooking, and other "nontraditional" topics. Classes generally meet once a week in the evenings. There are no grades, no exams, and no degrees. These programs are strictly for those who want to expand their knowledge in interesting, practical, and fun areas.

Below are names and phone numbers of adult learning centers around the country offering similar programs:

Center for Adult Education, Boston, MA www. bcae.org. 617-267-4430.

Discovery Center www.discoverycenter.cc. Chicago, Illinois. 773-348-8120.

Discovery Center. Oneonta, New York. 607-436-2011.

First Class. Washington, DC. 202-797-5102.

Mt. Airy Learning Tree www.mtairy.org. Philadelphia, Pennsylvania. 215-843-6333.

The Learning Annex www.thelearningannex.com is a national franchise with centers located in Los Angeles, San Diego, San Francisco and New York. Since it first began 10 years ago, 1.3 million students have attended more than 132,000 learning Annex classes. For information on Learning Annex courses contact: The Learning Annex, Corporate Office, 2330 Broadway, New York, NY 10024 or call the Learning Annex in one of the above cities.
New York Office: 212-371-0280
Los Angeles: 310-478-6677
San Francisco: 415-788-5500
San Diego: 619-544-9700

Auditing Seniors
Of all the travel privileges enjoyed by mature and senior citizens, one in particular is virtually unknown and largely unutilized, and yet it is the single most valuable of them all: The right to "audit" courses free of charge (or for a nominal sum) at dozens of state and city universities. Though housing is generally available only

in the summer, the free course privileges are offered throughout the year to seniors 60, 62 or 65 years of age and older (depending on the university), who then make their own housing arrangements for the non-summer months in motels or bed and breakfasts nearby.

Schools Admitting Seniors from Any State:

Boston University: The university's "Evergreen Program" permits senior citizens (60 and older) from anywhere to audit courses for $20 a course throughout the year. Currently, the university receives 200 to 300 senior auditors per semester, and does make some university housing available to them in summer. Write: The Evergreen Program, Boston University, 808 Commonwealth Avenue, Boston, MA 02215. Call 617-353-9852, or visit the web site: www.bu.edu/met/ programs/nondeg/evergreen/evergreen.html.

University of Connecticut: Seniors 62 and older can audit as many classes as they choose for a fee of $15 per semester, space available. No requirement of state residence, and housing is available in summer on a space available basis for $91 a week in dorms, $78.65 a week for a 15-meal plan. Phone 860-241-4724 for an application form to attend classes at the campuses either in West Hartford or Storrs, Connecticut.

University of Illinois: Persons 65 and older, from anywhere, can audit as many courses as they like (as long as they have the instructor's approval), other than labs or physical education classes, for a token fee of $15 per course (which run, in summer, for either four or eight weeks). But auditors have no university privileges (housing, meal plans), and must fend for themselves in that regard. Write: Office of Administration and Records, Room 100, Henry Administration Building, 901 West Illinois, Room 140, Urbana, IL 61801. 217-333-0302.

Eastern Kentucky University: Senior citizens from any state, 65 and older, may audit any course for free, under the terms of the O'Donnell Scholarship and enjoy university housing ($834 per semester for a single room) and meal plans ($860 per semester for 20 meals a week), along with library privileges. Write: Admissions Office, 203 Jones Building, Richmond KY 40475.

University of Massachusetts: By state law, seniors 60 and over, from any state, can take up to six credits per semester (or summer sessions) free of charge, and are entitled to rooms in dorms for $1319 per semester, plus a $50 registration fee. And they can sign on for 19 meals a week for $950 per semester. Write: Admissions Office, University of Massachusetts, Amherst, MA 01003. 413-545-0222.

University of Mississippi: "Mature citizens" from any state, 65 and older, can enroll for up to four credit hours per semester absolutely free, and can apply for university residence halls and meal plans on a space-available basis. One such applicant, in his late 70s, who feared his hearing wasn't up to par, was advised to tape lectures and later re-play what he failed to catch. The approach worked fine. Write:

Office of Admissions, University of Mississippi, University, MS 38677 or call 601-232-7226.

University of New Mexico: Seniors 65 and older can take classes (auditing or for credit) for $5 per credit hour. While they have library privileges, they have no on-campus housing or meal plans. Write: The Admissions Office, University of New Mexico, Albuquerque, NM 87131.

University of North Carolina: Non-matriculated students of any age, and from any state, can audit courses for $10 per course, if they have instructors' permission. Summer courses are presented in two, five-week sessions; but no assistance is given for housing or meals. Write: University of North Carolina at Chapel Hill, CB#3340, 200 Pettigrew Hall, Chapel Hill, NC 27599. Call the main operator at 919-962-2211, to connect you directly with the professor whose class you wish to take.

University of North Dakota: Seniors age 65 and older can audit classes for free (except art & science classes that may have a lab or materials fee). Although housing and meal plans aren't available to auditors, meals can be purchased by anyone at university dining halls. Write: Enrollment Services, Box 8135, University Station, Grand Forks, ND 58202.

Ohio State University: By command of the legislature, anyone 60 or older from any state can audit classes free of charge ("Program 60"), and there is no restriction on participation in class discussion. Currently, up to 200 seniors do so at any one time, by traveling to Columbus, Ohio, for five-week courses in summer, ten-week courses ("quarters") all other times; obviously, they can stay for less than five or ten weeks by dropping out before that time. Write: Office of Continuing Education, 152 Mount Hall, 1050 Carmack Road, Ohio State University, Columbus, OH 43210. Call 614-292-8860.

University of Oklahoma: Seniors 65 and older may audit courses free of charge, but have no access to university housing or meal plans. They must register within the first ten weeks of the semester, and then, only with the permission of the instructor. Write: Registration Office, Buchanan Hall, University of Oklahoma, 1000 Asp Avenue, Norman, OK 73109.

University of Wyoming: Persons 65 and older can take classes (even for credit) entirely free, depending on availability. And on-campus single rooms are available to them in summer at $720 for 8 weeks if they take at least 6 credits. Write: Division of Admissions, University of Wyoming, Box 3435, Laramie, WY 82071. 800-423-5809.

Schools Admitting State Residents Only:
University of Alaska: Persons 65 and older can take (for credit) or audit any course free of charge. They also receive library privileges, and—if enrolled for as many as 12 credit hours—housing privileges (whose

costs vary in different residence halls) and meal plans (three meals daily for an entire semester, $775). "Our student body is very impressed by persons in their mature age who wish to continue their education," says admissions officer Pamela Guzzy. Write: Admissions Office, P.O. Box 757480, University of Alaska, Fairbanks, AK 99775-7480, or call 907-474-6300.

University of Arkansas: Persons 60 and older can either audit or take courses for credit, free, and are eligible for university housing and meals if they take a full-course load. Single rooms with all three meals daily are $2009 per semester; singles without meals are $15.85 a day in summer-a good time to attend short courses. Call 501-575-5451, and request an advisor assigned by the Returning Students Association.

University of Colorado (at Boulder): At the Boulder campus only, state residents aged 55 and older can audit classes very inexpensively, but aren't eligible for campus housing or meal plans. Dues-paying members of the alumni association, which organizes these programs for the university, pay only $5 per class; nonmembers pay $35. The registrar with whom I spoke recalls overhearing an effort by an 18-year-old freshman to persuade a 70-year-old auditor not to drop a class they were attending together. Phone 303-492-8484, or write to The Senior Auditing Program, Coenig Alumni Center, Box 457, Boulder, CO 80309.

University of Delaware: State residents, 60 and older, can take as many classes as they choose, for free.

Non-residents joining the "Academy of Lifelong Learning" for an $80 a year charge, can audit one course, attend a separate lecture series, and participate in various social activities. Housing ($329 for five weeks) and meal plans ($395 for five weeks and three meals daily) are available only during a summer session of five and seven weeks' duration.

University of Georgia: Except at the law and medical schools, state residents 62 years of age and older can take up to three five-hour classes per semester (either for credit or as auditors) for free. They can also secure university housing for only $1,236 to $1,753 per quarter if they enroll in twelve or more hours of courses per week. Write: Office of Admissions, University of Georgia, Athens, GA 30602 or call 706-542-1421.

University of Hawaii: In the normal school year only (fall through spring), residents of the state 60 and older can visit classes, with instructors' permission, free of charge. They receive library privileges, as well, but aren't eligible for housing or meal plans. They aren't allowed to visit in summer. Write: Center for Adults Returning to Education, University of Hawaii at Manoa, 2600 Campus Road, SSC Room 413, Honolulu, HA 96822 or call 808-956-9317.

Idaho State University: Residents of Idaho, 60 and older, may audit by paying a flat fee of $20, plus $5 per credit—the average course consisting of three credits (i.e., three hours of instruction per week for one semester). Seniors are also eligible for university housing and meals: $2,190 for a single room throughout the entire year, all meals included. Write: Enrollment Management Services, Box 8054, Idaho State University, Pocatello, ID 83209. Call 208-236-0211.

University of Kansas: Persons 60 and over can audit as many courses as they wish, for free; but auditors aren't entitled to housing or meal plans. Call Office of Admissions: 785-864-4560.

University of Maryland: Under the "Golden I.D." program, seniors 60 and up can audit up to three courses at a time for about $150. While auditors aren't eligible for housing or meal plans, they do have library privileges. Write: Undergraduate Admissions, University of Maryland, The Mitchell Building, College Park, MD 20742.

University of Michigan: At the Dearborn campus only, the "Retired Persons Scholarship Program" permits residents of the state 60 and over, who must be retired, to audit or take up to 3 courses for a flat fee of $125. Over 300 such seniors are currently enrolled, most of them studying art, history and philosophy. At the school's Ann Arbor campus, seniors 65 and over receive a 50% discount off normal tuition fees. Write: Retired Persons Scholarship Program, University of Michigan, 4901 Evergreen Road, Dearborn, MI 48128 or call 313-593-5031.

University of Minnesota: State residents only, 62 or older, can audit classes for free at all state campuses throughout the year; they join each class on a space available basis after the first day of instruction. University housing? It's sometimes available, mainly in summer. Write: Admissions Office, University of Minnesota, 150 Williamson Hall, 231 Pillsbury Drive S.E., Minneapolis, MN 55455 or call 612-625-3333.

University of Montana: State residents 62 and older pay $19 per credit for most courses. Single rooms cost them only $1,177 per quarter; all three meals daily costs $1,222 per quarter. Write: Business Services Office, University of Montana, Missoula, MT 59812 or call 406-243-6266.

University of Nevada: Fall and spring semesters only, 62 and older, can audit courses free of charge; during summer sessions, oddly enough, they pay 50% (about $78 per credit) of the normal tuition charge. University housing ($1,825 a year, no meals) is available to senior citizens pursuing a minimum of twelve credits. Write: Office of Admissions Records, University of Nevada, Reno, NV 89557 or call 775-784-4865.

University of New Hampshire: Residents of the state, 65 and older, can take up to two courses at a time for free, by paying a single $15 registration fee. Library privileges, yes; housing or meal plans, no. Write: Department of the Registrar, 11 Garrison Avenue, University of New Hampshire, Durham, NH 03824 or call 603-862-1500.

State University of New York: At every one of its many campuses, state residents 55 and older can audit classes (other than language or lab courses) free of charge, but only during the standard school year, and not in summer. Library privileges are also granted, but not housing or meal plans. Write to the branch you desire to attend, for instance, Office of General Studies, State U. at Albany, 1400 Washington Avenue, Room LI85, Albany, NY 12222. 578-443-5555.

University of Rhode Island: State residents only, 60 and older, are entitled to a waiver of all tuition charges other than a $20 registration, $20 activities fee and a $4 per credit fee (that goes towards library and computer services), but receive no housing or meal plans. Write: The College of Continuing Education, University of Rhode Island, 199 Promenade Street, Providence, RI 02908. Call them at 401-874-1000.

University of South Carolina: State residents age 60 and up who are retired can attend classes free of charge, and rent a double room in university residences for the entire year, for $2700 per person, including all three meals a day. Write: Adult Student Services, 900 Assembly Street, University of South Carolina, Columbia SC 29208.

University of Utah: Residents 62 and older can audit as many classes as they care to, for a flat $25 fee per quarter (business management classes, art classes and labs excepted). They can also use the library and computer center for free, and the gymnasium and all other recreational facilities for an activities fee of $2.50 per quarter. Housing assistance isn't provided. Write: Lifespan Learning, University of Utah, 1195 Annex, Salt Lake City, UT 84112 or call 801-581-3228.

University of Tennessee: Auditing of courses is free to seniors 60 and older. They receive library privileges, too, but no housing or meal plans. Write: Evening School Offices (which administers the program for all other divisions), 451 Communications Building, University of Tennessee, Knoxville, TN 37996 or call 801-656-3480.

University of Vermont: Holders of the "Green Mountain Pass" (available from any town clerk in Vermont), who are 65 or older, receive free tuition for as many classes as they choose, and are also eligible for on-campus housing ($1493 per semester) and meals ($808 per semester). "Younger students love the benefit of having elderly people in the class," says the school's registrar. Write: Continuing Education, 322 South Prospect, University of Vermont, Burlington, VT 05405 or call 802-656-3480.

University of Virginia: State residents only, 60 and older who have taxable incomes of less than $10,000, can audit up to three courses for free during summer sessions and the school year. Single rooms are also made available to them for $75 a week. Write: The Summer Session, 210 Miller Hall, University of Virginia, Charlottesville VA 22903.

Travel and Learn

Mature adults are among the largest percentage of national and international travelers. They also enjoy learning while they travel. As a result there are several extensive college campus and learning programs available worldwide that are tailored as learning experiences for seniors:

The Earthwatch Institute www.earthwatch.org. E-mail info@earthwatch.org. PO Box 9104, Watertown, MA 02272. 617-926-8200 or 800-776-0188. The Earthwatch Institute sends its volunteers on scientific research projects (tagging turtles, measuring acid rain, interviewing rural residents), making use of a catch-as-catch-can array of housing accommodations (local schools and community centers, tents, and private homes) in which people are lodged as conditions permit.

Elderhostel www.elderhostel.org. Each year over 270,000 people fill classrooms all over the United States and around the world through Elderhostel, a nonprofit organization with the philosophy that education can be fulfilling and fun. Elderhostel has one- and two-week programs at more than 2,000 colleges, universities, research stations, and other educational institutions around the globe. Each offers low-cost sessions for people 55 years and older.

Classes are a blend of lectures, cultural events, local exploration, and social activity. They cover such diverse subjects as local history and culture, archaeology, the sciences, arts, and literature. The Elderhostel catalog is produced seasonally and filled with fascinating, enticing programs. I discovered the catalog at my local library and spent several hours poring over its wonderful courses.

The organization has begun adding brand-new "service programs" that take mature idealists to perform Peace Corps-like activities in emerging nations, or to conduct academic research in the environmental area, or to build low-cost housing in communities of the United States. While none of the latter projects breaks new ground, they enable mature persons to perform these tasks in the company of people their age. Initial responses to the new offerings have been strong.

The cost of Elderhostel is intentionally held to modest levels, consistent with traditional hostelling philosophy. Accommodations are simple and the food wholesome and nutritious. At approximately $350 a week, plus transportation, Elderhostel remains a stunning value and an inspiring opportunity for every mature American. If the cost is still prohibitive for you or someone you know, check on the "Hostelship" scholarship program which pays all expenses for those who meet the requirements.

As it continues to grow, this fine organization offers hope that the mature population of America will become the single best-informed, and therefore most influential, segment of our society. For information or to book a course, write Elderhostel, 75 Federal Street, Boston, MA 02110 or call 877-426-8056.

Interhostel is an international study-travel program for energetic people over 50. Sponsored by the University of New Hampshire, Interhostel offers two-week "educational experiences" at colleges and universities in Europe, China, and Australia. Programs combine lessons in history and culture with lectures, field trips, and social activities.

As with the Elderhostel program, costs are kept moderate. Included are two weeks full room and board, tuition, and ground transportation. For information write: Interhostel, University of New Hampshire, 6 Garrison Ave., Durham, NH 03824. 800-733-9753.

Northeastern Senior Seminars www.skidmore.edu. These are a series of one-week summer residential seminars given at several New York universities. You must be 55 or older to be eligible for the programs. A wide range of courses is offered along with side trips to places of interest in the surrounding areas. Participants live in dorms and are given three meals a day for approximately $300 per week. There are also commuter rates. Contact: Summer Special Programs, Skidmore College, Saratoga Springs, NY 12866 for information.

Senior Ventures www.cwu.edu. Sponsored by Central Washington University, this program offers two- and four-week Senior Ventures sessions. Seniors participate in in-class learning, class-related excursions, and just-for-the-fun-of-it explorations of Washington State. For information: Senior Ventures, Central Washington University, Ellensburg, WA 98926. 509-963-2127.

Language Study Abroad www.languagestsudy. com. Since 1987, Language Study Abroad has presented highly professional "total immersion" language study programs in Mexico, Spain, France and Italy. Their goal is to have students become conversationally fluent as soon as possible in the languages of the country. Each program offers classes in small groups at all levels throughout the year. All of the instructors are native-born and educated in their respective countries. Housing is arranged with carefully selected local families to expose the student to the people and the culture, and to offer unlimited conversational practice.

Seniors, especially, are an important part of their program, since they often are the ones who have the time and desire to learn another language at this time of their lives. In addition, all ages of students come from universities, high schools, government agencies and international corporations to participate in this highly qualified and recommended program. For more information write them at: Language Study Abroad, 1960 5th Avenues, San Rafael, CA 94901. 415-454-9072 or visit their comprehensive web site at: www.languagestudy.com.

They also offer similar programs in Spanish in Seville, Spain, and in French in Vichy, France. For information on tours write: Senior Study Center— Language Study Abroad, 130l N. Maryland Ave., Glendale, CA 91207.

Go to the Head of the Class

North Carolina Center for Creative Retirement (NCCCR) ww.unca.edu/nccr. The purpose of the center is to help enrich the lives of retirement-age people and, in fact, benefit Americans of all generations through educational and cultural programs. Eight programs are offered for those over 50 looking for ways to build fulfilling lives for themselves and others. The programs include: Senior Leadership Seminars in history, culture, politics, economics, and social structure; the Retirement Wellness Center for training seniors to be wellness advocates in their community; The College for Seniors, where classes are free from the pressures of testing and grades; Retirement Issues Forum; The Research Institute; the Retirement Planning Program; and The Senior Academy for Intergenerational Learning, where retired experts work with undergraduates. Contact: The North Carolina Center for Creative Retirement, 116 Rhoades Hall, Asheville, NC 28804-3299. 828-251-6140.

Close Up Foundation www.closeup.org. For those 50 and older the Program for Older Americans provides up close, behind-the-scenes educational tours of Washington, DC, and other places. The purpose is to give individuals a first-hand look at how government functions in our capital city. Activities include walks on Capitol Hill, seminars with key Washington personalities, bus tours, workshops and briefings on current events and issues, and social activities. These one-week programs give seniors a great opportunity to enhance their knowledge about our country's political process. Contact: Close Up Foundation, Program for Older Americans, 44 Canal Center Plaza, Alexandria, Virginia 22314-1592. 703-706-3579.

University Seniors ww.uregina.ca. E-mail: seniors@ uregina.ca. New York University offers people over 65 two free university courses per semester and biweekly luncheon discussions on current events and topics of interest. Contact: University Seniors, 251 Darland Administration Building, 101 University Drive, Duluth, MN 55812-2496. 218-726-7637. Locations include: Colorado (303-315-7851) and Canada—University of Regina, GA 106 Gallery Building, College Avenue and Cornwall Street, Regina, Saskatchewan, Canada S4S OA2. 306-585-5816.

"Go-60" Program www.outreach.psu.edu. Pennsylvania State University will give college credit courses at half tuition for seniors over 60 who are retired or employed less than half-time and are current residents of Pennsylvania, former Penn State students, or former Penn State employees. Contact: Independent Learning Office, Pennsylvania State University, 118 Keller Building, University Park, PA 16802-1300. 814-863-1738.

The Smithsonian Institution www.si.edu. The Resident Associate Program (RAP), a privately supported membership arm of The Smithsonian Institution, presents a wide variety of enriching education opportunities including cultural activities and public outreach programs. Resident members receive advance notice of programs and significantly reduced admittance fees for performing arts programs, lectures, films, seminars, studio arts, and courses. Contact the Resident Associate Program, The Smithsonian Institution, Washington D.C. 20560. 202-357-3030.

Chautauqua Institution www.chautauqua-inst. org. This institution sponsors summer weekends and one-week programs for folks over 55 at an 856-acre site on the shore of Lake Chautauqua, New York. A wide variety of educational programs with discussions, workshops, lectures, films, evening entertainment, and recreational activities are offered at this relatively inexpensive adult summer camp. Fees cover tuition, room, meals, and activities. For information write: Program Center of Older Adults, P.O. Box 28, One Ames Avenue, Chautauqua, NY 14722. 800-836-ARTS.

The College at 60—New York City www.fordham. edu. The Lincoln Center campus of Fordham University offers credit college courses in liberal arts subjects taught by Fordham faculty members. Actually available to adults over 50, the program includes a lecture series and use of all campus facilities. Contact: The College at 60, Fordham University at Lincoln Center, 113 W. 60th St., New York, NY 10023. Bronx Location: 441 East Fordham Road, Bronx, New York 10458.

Duquesne University offers senior citizens over 60 discounts for full- or part-time study for one degree. For information write: Duquesne University, Office of Admissions, Pittsburgh, PA 15282.

The Educational network for Older Adults www. enoa.org. A network of 65 colleges and universities, adult organizations, community centers, and associations in Chicago whose purpose is to help older people find educational and training programs. The ENOA Resource

Center offers free information, vocational programs, job assistance programs, educational programs, financial-retirement seminars, business opportunities for older adults, etc. Contact: The Educational Network for Older Adults, 36 S. Wabash. Suite 624, Chicago, IL 60603.

Elder College at Hofstra. Located in Hempstead, New York, this is a series of one-week (Mon.–Fri.) commuter programs for people over 60 covering a variety of cultural and historical subjects. For information write: Elder College al. Hofstra, UCCE, 232 Memorial Hall, Hempstead, NY 11550.

SeniorNet www.seniornet.org is a nonprofit organization that provides adults 50 and over with an education on how computer technologies and the Internet can enhance their lives and enable them to share their knowledge and wisdom. This program originated at the University of San Francisco as a research project to study the use of computer communication networking by older adults. Members throughout the United States and Canada communicate with one another and gain access to information of interest to them.

SeniorNet currently sponsors over 170 Learning Centers around the country for training, networking, and sociability. They also offer computer classes designed especially for older adults. There are more than 34,000 SeniorNet members linked by a national on-line computer network. Membership includes a quarterly newsletter, discounts on bard ware and software products, a discounted registration to the annual SeniorNet conference, and a copy of the book, *Computers for Kids over Sixty*. Members pay a one-time fee to set up a network account (monthly subscription fees and hourly rates are extra). Members learn and teach others to use computers and communications technologies to accomplish a variety of tasks. They learn to desktop publish anything from a newsletter to an autobiography, manage personal and financial records, communicate with others across the country and the world and serve their communities.

SeniorNet operates SeniorNet Online on America Online (keyword: SeniorNet) and their own web site www.seniornet.org, where all individuals 50 and older, whether they are or are not members of SeniorNet, are welcome to participate in the hundreds of discussion topics offered on these sites. For information contact: SeniorNet, 121 Second Street, 7th Floor, San Francisco, California 94105. 415-495-4990.

Stress-Free Learning

There are several programs throughout the country affiliated with colleges, universities, and learning institutes that offer senior or adult oriented stress-free (no grades, no tests) classes. The courses are led by professionals who offer their expertise on a wide variety of subjects. Students pay an annual fee to the sponsoring university and may take as many courses as they wish (some also charge a reduced fee for individual courses). Included are campus privileges and use of campus facilities. Contact the individual campuses listed below for details on their programs:

Academy of Lifelong Learning. www.udel.edu. University of Delaware, 2800 Pennsylvania Ave., CED, Wilmington, DE 19806. 302-573-4417.

Center for Creative Retirement. 116 Rhoades Hall, Asheville, NC 28804-3299. 828-251-6140.

Center for Learning in Retirement www.ucop. edu. University of California Extension Center, 55 Laguna St., San Francisco, CA 94102. 415-476-9000.

Duke Institute for Learning in Retirement www. learnmore.duke.edu. E-mail: Scraven@duke.edu. Duke Continuing Education, Box 90704, Durham, North Carolina 27708.

Educational Growth Opportunities(EGO) www. sdsu.edu. College of Extended Studies, San Diego State University, 5500 Campanile Drive, San Diego, CA 92182. 619-594-5200.

Learning Center www.icmarc.org. E-mail: customerservice@icmarc.org. Home of the Public Sector Retirement Specialists. 800-669-7400.

The Harvard Institute for Learning in Retirement www.harvard.edu. Lehman Hall B-3, Cambridge, MA 02138.

The Institute for Learning in Retirement www.northwestern.edu. Northwestern 4, 2115 N. Campus Drive, STE 162, Evanston, Illinois 60208.

Institute for Retired Professionals. Syracuse University, 700 University Avenue, Syracuse, New York 13244-2530. 315-443-4846.

New York Location: 66 West 12th St, New York, New York 10011. 212-229-5682. www.newschool.edu.

Miami Location: University of Miami, P.O. Box 248276, Coral Gables, Florida 33124-2422. 305-284-5072. www.coralgables.net

Institute of New Dimensions. Palm Beach Junior College, Central (Lake Worth) Campus, 4200 Congress Avenue, Lake Worth, Florida 33461. 561-439-8186.

Nova College Institute for Retired Professionals www.nova.edu. 3301 College Avenue, Fort Lauderdale, Florida 33314-7796. 800-541-6682.

The Plato Society of UCLA www.unex.ucla.edu. University of California at Los Angeles, 1083 Gayley Ave., Los Angeles, California 90024. 310-794-0231.

Professionals and Executives in Retirement www.hofstra.edu. Hofstra University, 1000 Hempstead Turnpike, Hempstead, NY 11550.

CHAPTER 6

Here's to Your Health

No one will argue that our bodies begin to go through changes after the age of 50. These changes are as normal and natural as anything else in our lives. At the same time, remaining strong, fit, and healthy will allow us to enjoy all the wonderful benefits of being a senior. Below are sources of information and preventive care to help you maintain the highest quality of health— your most precise commodity—throughout your life.

Since maintaining and improving health is such an important, universal concern, many dedicated individuals, groups, and nonprofit organizations offer free or low-cost testing, screening, and information on a variety of health concerns specifically related to the needs of older Americans.

Even with Medicare, Medicaid, and the numerous supplemental medical insurance plans, costs for preventive tests and exams are not always affordable. However, there are public and private facilities offer screenings, health assessments, and health education sessions as a public service. Look for advertisements for these screenings in the lifestyle section of your local newspaper. Some hospitals and medical facilities send out newsletters and mailings announcing times and dates of free medical testing for seniors. Check senior newspapers for calendar listings and ads on upcoming testing dates.

Many national associations, organizations, foundations, and manufacturers of medical equipment designate certain times of the year as "National _____ Prevention Month." For example, May is "Better Hearing and Speech Month," September is "National Breast Cancer Month," "Adult Immunization Week" comes at the end of October, and there is even an "Osteoporosis Prevention Week." During these designated weeks and months, vigorous campaigns and programs are implemented nationwide to create awareness of techniques of early testing and treatment for practically every illness from the flu to breast cancer.

Announcements of free and low-cost clinics associated with these yearly campaigns are usually made through local newspapers and publications.

Some companies use their medical departments or work with community agencies and local hospitals to provide a wide variety of screenings to determine employees' risk for developing certain diseases. Blood pressure screenings are the most common, but more comprehensive testing of blood and cholesterol levels are becoming available. Some companies will even provide follow up sessions with company doctors. This form of preventative care saves thousands of dollars in anticipated medical costs to companies offering medical insurance and coverage to employees.

There are also medical manufacturing companies that offer mobile testing services at local pharmacies, markets, shopping malls, health fairs, and health expos. Screenings include vision and hearing exams, pediatric exams, diabetic and glucose tolerance tests, mammograms, general dental screenings, body composition, pulmonary function tests, blood pressure, cholesterol, and stroke detection tests. Here is an example of a recent announcement in a newspaper "Check your blood pressure at the Beach Cities health District Health Fair on the Hermosa Beach Pier Plaza. The free fair offers 15 screenings, including tests for skin cancer and bone density, vision and hearing. You can also donate blood and learn about clinical trials and women's health." Be on the lookout for such announcements in your local newspaper.

Books and Information on Health

The National Institute on Aging (NIA) www. nih.gov offers free publications covering many areas of health and aging. Some of their titles include: "Accidental Hypothermia," "Exercise Packet, Nutrition Packet," "Resource Directory for Older People," "The Menopause Time of Life," "What Is Your Aging IQ?," and "Women's Age Page Packet."

Of special interest to women is the guide entitled "Health Resources for Older Women," a 75-page booklet that describes the normal changes that take place during the aging process as well as conditions like arthritis and osteoporosis that become more prevalent in later years. The booklet provides a useful introduction to the challenges that mature women face (including financial planning, care giving, housing options, and widowhood) and offers good tips on ways to deal with them.

The NIA also publishes a series called "Age Pages," which provide a quick, practical look at health topics that interest older people. There are over forty "Age Pages" covering the following areas:

Diseases and Disorders; Health Promotion; Medical Care; Medications; Nutrition; Safety; Your Aging Body.

Write to The National Institute on Aging, Information Center, Building 31, 31 Center Drive, MSC, Bethesda, MD 20892 for a complete list of their free publications or call 301-496-1752.

The Consumer Information Center, P.O. Box 100, Pueblo, CO 81002 publishes a quarterly "Consumer Information Catalog." This is a wonderful catalog that lists over 200 titles, covering a variety of practical, useful subjects such as drugs and health aids, medical problems, mental health, and general health. Examples of some current titles include:

"Dizziness"; "The Menopause Time of Life"; "Facing Surgery"; "Do-It-Yourself Medical Testing"; "The Colon"; "Food and Drug Interactions"; "Gallstones"; "Some Things You Should Know About Prescription Drugs"; "Heart Attacks"; "Osteoporosis". Call them at 800-688-9889 or 1-800-8 PUEBLO. Web site: www.pueblo.gsa.gov.

The FDA Consumer is a publication by the U.S. Food and Drug Administration www.fda.gov. It provides information and reports on new medicines, their benefits and side effects, health advice of special concern to the elderly, and discussions of topics like sodium, osteoporosis, and generic drugs. The FDA Consumer is the official magazine of the FDA, which serves as the consumer protection agency responsible for food, drugs, medical devices, and other products used in daily life. Write: FDA Consumer, Superintendent of Documents, Washington DC 20402.

Write the American College of Surgeons, Office of Public Information, 633 North Saint Clair St, Chicago, Illinois 60611 for a free booklet on "When You Need an Operation." Web site: www.facs.org. E-mail: Postmaster@facs.org.

For free information on high blood pressure and diet write the High Blood Pressure Information Center, 120/80, National Institutes of Health, Box AP, Bethesda, MD 20892. Web site: www.nih.gov.

The National Heart, Lung and Blood Institute (NHLBI) www.nhibi.nih.gov/nhlbi/nhlbi.htm conducts research and answers questions on cholesterol, blood resources, obesity, asthma, high blood pressure, and sleep disorders. They also distribute a variety of educational publications for consumers and professionals. Contact them for a free catalog of their publications: National Near, Lung and Blood Institute Information

Center, PO Box 30105, Bethesda, MD 20824-0105. 800-575-WELL.

The American Heart Association www.american heart.org publishes free reports and brochures covering all types of heart disease. They offer a variety of positive/ preventative tips for maintaining a healthy cardiovascular system. For a list of publications write: American Heart Association, National Center, 7272 Greenville Avenue, Dallas, TX 75231, or contact your local chapter of the American Heart Association. 800-AHA-USA1.

Diabetes is a challenging, but controllable disease. The more you know about this disease that affects millions of Americans, the more you can prepare and live a healthy lifestyle that will insure you enjoy life to the fullest. The National Diabetes Clearinghouse will furnish you with loads of information from early warning signs to diet and food preparation. You can get a complete list of their publications from their web site at www.niddk.nih.gov or write them at: Clearinghouse at National Diabetes Information Clearinghouse, 1 Information Way, Bethesda, MD 20892-3560.

Even with all the information available on aging, many older people, their caregivers, and families have trouble finding the right information when they need it most.

The national Senior Helpline www.byu.edu was developed by the Gerontology Resource Center at

Brigham Young University as a free service with answers on subjects ranging from family and finances to health and housing. By calling a toll-free number, seniors in all 50 states and Puerto Rico can hear short messages that are easily understood, interesting, and informative.

For example, a caller concerned about health problems can listen to messages on Alzheimer's disease, alcoholism, bladder control, blood pressure, nutrition, and osteoporosis. There is also a free directory which, in addition to listing the message topics, includes names and addresses of foundations and professional organizations that can provide in-depth help on selected topics.

One of the benefits of the Helpline is the complete privacy in which a caller can listen to a message on a topic they may not wish to share with others. The toll-free number for the directory of messages and access codes is: 800-328-7576. To obtain a written directory write: BYU Senior Helpline, Brigham Young University; Provo, Utah 84602. Or call 800-378-INFO.

Health Newsletters

Although there are several health newsletters available to the general public published by educational institutions, the *John Hopkins Medical Letter: Health After 50*, is the first health newsletter specifically targeted for this age group. It is available from the Johns Hopkins Medical Institution, Dept. P, 550 N, Broadway, Suite 1100, Baltimore, MD 21205.

In addition, a growing number of companies and corporations are communicating health information to older workers and retirees through company newsletters and special mailings. Bank of America and Levi Strauss are two examples of companies that provide their retirees with free newsletters and self-help books containing information on health promotion and maintenance. The Center for Corporate Health Promotion, one of the Travelers Companies, has developed a series of materials that address the concerns of older adults. For information on these materials write: George J. Pfeiffer, Center for Corporate Health Promotion, Reston, VA.

More and more large community medical centers, teaching institutions and university medical centers are publishing informative and interesting community health newsletters. They include articles about testing programs, results of research studies, tips on maintaining health, articles on specific diseases or common conditions and dietary news and healthy lifestyle recipes. If you have a large hospital or community medical center nearby, give them a call and talk to their community relations department about getting on their mailing list.

National Organizations and Prevention Programs

Many national organizations provide free information on specific areas of health and disease prevention. Since many of these conditions begin to appear when we are older, I've included groups that offer materials on the more common health problems of mature adults.

The American Rheumatism Association www. rheumatology.org offers information, brochures, and background publications on arthritis and other related conditions. Write: American Rheumatism Association, 1800 Century Place, Suite 250, Atlanta, Georgia 30345. 404-633-3777 or 800-638-3030.

If you or a relative have arthritis and want more information, write to: The Arthritis Foundation, 1330 West Peachtree street, Atlanta, GA 30309. The foundation has 70 chapters throughout the United States that offer courses and support resources designed to help arthritis patients and their families. 800-283-7800. Web site: www.arthritis.org.

The National Jewish Center For Immunology and Respiratory Diseases www.njc.org will send you free brochures and publications by writing: Public Relations, National Jewish Center, 1400 Jackson Street, Denver, CO 80206. Or call 1-800-222-LUNG.

Blue Shield of California www.blueshieldca.com has a Senior Healthtrack program included with their Blue Shield Medicare Supplement plan. This is a computerized health management program with recommendations for staying healthy. For free information write: Mike 0dom/Public Relations, Blue Shield of California, Two North Point, San Francisco, CA 94133. 800-488-8000.

The National Osteoporosis Foundation, 1625 Eye Street, NW, Suite 822, Washington, DC 20006, provides booklets and information regarding this disease, which is most prevalent in older women. In addition,

Physical Therapy Services of Washington, DC, Inc. has produced the Osteoporosis Exercise Booklet describing easy-to-do exercises designed to increase bone mass. Write to Physical Therapy Services of Washington, DC, Inc., 1232 22nd St, NW, Washington, D.C. 20037-1292. 202-223-2226. Web site: www.nof.org.

The U.S. Department of Health and Human Services www.hhs.gov administers a special funding program called the Hill-Burton Program, which requires hospitals and health facilities to provide services to people unable to pay. Those services are available to anyone residing in the facility's area. For information on the program, write your regional office of the Department of Health and Human Services or call the hotline toll free number: 800-638-0742 or 202-619-0257.

The National Digestive Diseases Education and Information Clearinghouse, Box NDDIC, Bethesda, MD 20892 offers free information on this subject.

Other national associations that provide free consumer health information include:
American Diabetes Association, National Service Center, 1701 North Beauregard Street, Alexandria, VA 22311. 800-342-2383. Web site: www.diabetes.org.

Alzheimer's Association, 70 East Lake Street, Chicago, IL 60601. 800-621-0379. Although there is no cure or way to prevent the devastating effects of the progressive disease of Alzheimer's, there is an increasing amount of research being done on the subject in an attempt to find definitive causes and cures. The National Institute on Aging funds 28 Alzheimer's Disease Centers (ADC's) at major medical centers around the country. These institutions offer free diagnosis and treatment for volunteers for their research programs. If you know someone who might benefit from treatment, contact the medical college, university or medical institution in your area and inquire whether they provide services for Alzheimer's Disease research volunteers.

Alzheimer's Disease Education and Referral Center (part of the National Institute on Aging) www. alzheimers.org provides information on all aspects of Alzheimer's disease. They also have a database which includes references to patient and professional materials. Alzheimer's Disease Education and Referral Center, PO Box 8250, Silver Spring, MD 20907. 800-438-4380.

The Alzheimer's Association www.alz.org provides information, referrals and support services to patients and families as well as training for caregivers. For a list of chapters around the nation, call the national help line 800-272-3900.

The Family Caregiver Alliance www.caregiver.org, which offers Alzheimer's training programs for families and health care workers, also has presentations on dementia and approaches to care. Call 415-434-3388.

National Kidney Foundation, 2 Park Avenue, New York, NY, 10003. 212-889-2210. Web site: www.kidney.org.

National Mental Health Association, 1021 Prince Street, Alexandria, VA 22314. 703-604-7722.

In addition, some large university medical centers or community hospitals offer free membership programs, which include a variety of free services. For example, in Los Angeles, the UCLA Healthcare 50 Plus program helps people 50 and older maintain a healthy and independent lifestyle through a host of special benefits.

Additionally, the St. Johns Medical Center in Santa Monica, CA has Senior TLC (Teaching Lifestyle Changes), a free membership program for adults 50 years and older, dedicated to helping seniors manage their health and wellness. Recent program activities included: Seniorobics, Tai Chi Chuan, Stroke Support Group, Walking Group, Bingo, Blood Pressure Screenings, Senior TLC Self-Care clinic, Art Classes, All About Long Term Insurance, Women's Breast Conference, Tea and Travel. All About Retirement Planning, Healthy Cooking for the Holidays, and Senior TLC Annual Craft Fare.

These are extremely valuable and important services that are available completely free of charge. If you live in a metropolitan area or have a large university health center nearby, check to see if they offer any programs such as the one above.

Don't Lose Your Sight

For most of us our eyesight has already begun to change and may continue to change throughout our later years. In addition to changes in vision, more than 90 percent of Americans over 65 develop cataracts— but they vary in seriousness, and only a small percentage require surgery. Recent research has shown that drugs (including simple aspirin, and certain vitamins) may help prevent and significantly reduce a person's risk of developing cataracts. Some studies have even linked smoking and prolonged exposure to the sun to the risk of developing this condition. For free information send a self-addressed business-size envelope to the Inquiry Clerk in Department CT, the American Academy of Opthalmology, PO Box 7424, San Francisco, CA 94120-7424. 415-561-8500. Web site: www.eyenet.org.

The Vision Foundation, 2818 Mt. Auburn Street, Watertown, MA 02172 will send you a free "Vision Inventory List."

The National Society to Prevent Blindness, 500 East Remington Road, Schaumburg, IL 60178 has a free booklet called, "The Aging Eye: Facts on Eye Care for Older Persons."

The MD Foundation offers resources for information on macular degeneration. Write: PO Box 9752, San Jose, California 95157. 888-633-3937. Web site: www.eyesight.org.

Pearlvision Seniors Choice Program. Customers who are 50–59 years of age receive a 50 percent discount on the full retail price of their frames or lenses (the discount applies to the less expensive item) when purchasing a complete pair of glasses. There are over 850 Pearlevision locations across the United States and Canada. Call 800-282-3931 to find out where the nearest Pearlevision location is to you. Other discounts:

Seniors 60–69 receive a 60% discount.

Seniors 70–79 receive a 70% discount.

Seniors 80–89 receive an 80% discount.

Seniors 90–99 receive a 90% discount.

Seniors 100+ years of age receive frames or lenses at no cost.

Visit the web site at www.pearlevision.com.

The National Eye Institute (NEI) www.nei.hih. gov conducts research on prevention, treatment, diagnosis and disorders of the eye. They publish free booklets including: "Cataracts," "Don't Lose Sight of Glaucoma," "Don't Lose Sight of Cataracts," "Don't Lose Sight of Age-Related Macular Degeneration," "Don't Lose Sight of Diabetic Eye Disorders," "Diabetic Retinopathy." Write them at National Eye Institute, Information Office, Building 31, Room 6A32, 31 Center Dr. MSC 2510, Bethesda, MD 20892-2510.

The Glaucoma Foundation has a very interesting and informative web site, www.glaucoma-foundation. org where you can learn the best ways to prevent blindness and receive good eye care. You can also write them at: 33 Maiden Lane, New York, NY 10038 for free information on eye care and prevention of glaucoma.

Keeping Your Skin Healthy

Another highly treatable problem that often does not show up until later in life is skin cancer. Since it sometimes takes 20 or more years to develop following overexposure to the sun, skin cancer's incidence increases with age.

May is "National Skin Cancer & Detection Month." The American Academy of Dermatology www.aad.org can tell you which doctors in your area are giving free screenings. Call them at 888-462-DERM or look for announcements in senior newspapers. Or check directly with the health facilities, clinics, and hospitals in your area for when they conduct low-cost or free exams.

In California, The Skin Cancer Institute www.cdc.gov/cancer, 800-842-6365, offers free examinations for senior citizens 62 or older, or for anyone of any age with previous skin cancer. The Cancer Detection Center, a nonprofit corporation operating in Los Angeles since 1944, conducts periodic free skin cancer exams along with low-cost physical examinations for both men and women.

What You Should Know About Breast Cancer

The National Breast Cancer Screening Consortium offers a free informational brochure by sending a self-addressed stamped envelope to PO Box 4333, Grand Central Station, New York, NY 10163-4333. The American Cancer Society www.cancer.org actively promotes nationwide low-cost mammogram programs during the year, especially in October during National Breast Cancer Awareness Month. Call: 800-ACS-2345.

Private and public health facilities cooperate with these screening and information programs. The National Alliance of Breast Cancer Organizations www.nabco.org has over 220 member organizations around the country. They function as a resource network by sending out free pamphlets and articles and referring individuals to their members for consultation, screening, and information. If you have any questions write them at: National Alliance of Breast Cancer Organizations, 9 East 37th Street, New York, NY 10016. 212-889-0606.

Finally, the National Cancer Institute publishes an informative 52-page booklet entitled, "Understanding Breast Changes." They also publish several booklets on other topics related to cancer including nutrition, detection, prevention, smoking, surviving cancer and more. Visit their web site at www.nci.nih.gov or call them toll free at 800-4-CANCER.

Pay Attention to Your Prostrate

Many men past the age of 40 develop prostate disorders, which in most cases are treatable with a simple outpatient procedure. In Los Angeles, The Brotman Medical Center offers free prostate screenings. Call the medical centers in your area to see it they offer similar screenings. The address for the Brotman Medical Center is: 3828 Delmas Terrace, Culver City, California 90237. 310-836-7000.

The National Kidney and Urologic Diseases Information Clearinghouse publishes a series of free publications on this subject. Titles include: *Age Page:*

Prostate Problems and *Prostate Enlargement: Benign Prostatic Hyperplasia.* Write them at: National Kidney and Urologic Diseases Information Clearinghouse, 3 Information Way, Bethesda, MD 20891-3580. Check out the web site at: www.niddk.nih.gov.

Don't Boo-Hoo the Flu

Another common concern among older adults is the flu. A yearly vaccine for seniors 55 and older is highly recommended, as well as a one-time dose of pneumonia vaccine. The idea that you can develop some kind of natural and lasting immunity to influenza is not true since flu viruses do change from year to year. The current vaccine has keen proven to be very safe and effective about 80 percent of the time, greatly decreasing the risks of complications from flu.

Free and low-cost flu shots are provided by dozens of county health departments, health maintenance organizations, nursing homes, and community centers. They are given at grocery stores, drug stores, local hospitals, senior centers, parks, banks, and other public sites. For example, FHP Health Care provides free shots at various FHP Centers.

The National Coalition for Adult Immunization (NCAI) has a public education program that begins during Adult Immunization Week in October of each year. Booklets and information sheets are available through the NCAI, National Foundation for Infectious Diseases, 4733 Bethesda Ave., Suite 750, Bethesda, MD 20814.

A free 12-page pamphlet titled "Immunization of Adults: A Call to Action" and a "Lifetime Personal

Immunization Record" are available from the Center for Disease Control, Center For Prevention Services, Division of Immunization, Atlanta, GA 30333.

A free publication entitled, *Flu*, is published by the National Institute of Allergy and Infectious Diseases, Office of Communications Building 31, Room 7A50, 31 Center Dr. MSC 2520, Bethesda, MD 20892-2520. Check out the web site www.niaid,nih.gov for more information.

Taking Care of Your Teeth

Dental problems and tooth loss do not have to be serious issues for older people. In fact, losing teeth is not a normal part of aging. Over 60 percent of people 65 and older have their natural teeth. However, it is necessary to continue regular check-ups and treatment throughout your life. It has been proven that good oral health can affect and actually improve overall health. Unfortunately, Medicare does not pay for most dental care, and few older persons have separate dental insurance. This means the vast majority of dental services received are paid for out-of-pocket.

One way to reduce the high cost of dental care is through treatment at one of the 57 accredited dental schools in this country and Canada. Most of them provide patient care at 50 percent or more off most services. Many also provide special free services for the community-at-large, such as care to nursing home patients, oral cancer screenings at senior centers, and staff training to consumer groups. In addition, recent federal legislation has made the 15,000 nursing homes in this country receiving federal dollars directly responsible for the dental care needs of their residents.

There are over 200 dental hygiene programs across the country that provide special services for older persons. Many state and local health departments support dental clinics that offer their services for free or payment basis. Services are usually restricted to those with limited income or special needs. To find out about a dental care or research programs in your area contact your local dental society (listed in the phone book) or write one of the following:

American Association of Dental Schools www. aads.jhu.edu. 1625 Massachusetts Avenue, NW, Washington, DC 20036-2212. 202-667-9433. E-mail: ADEA@adea.org.

American Dental Association www.ada.org. 211 East Chicago Avenue Chicago, IL 60611.

American Society for Geriatric Dentistry. 211 East Chicago Avenue, 16th Floor Chicago, IL 60611. 312-440-2500.

National Institute of Dental and Craniofacial Research. 31 Center Dr., MSC 2190, Build. 31 Room 5B49, Bethesda, MD 20892-2190.

Help for Hearing

The following are sources of free and low-cost hearing exams:

To find a otolaryngologist (ear, nose, and throat doctor), or otologist (ear-only specialist), write to:

Physician's List, American Academy of Otolaryngology, Head and Neck Surgery www.oto-online.org. One Prince St., Alexandria, VA 22314. Enclose a SASE to receive a free list of doctors in your area. 330-492-2844.

If you think you might have a hearing problem, you can contact Self Help For Hard of Hearing People (SHHH) www.shhh.org. They offer low cost publications on dealing with hearing problems and a list of 200 support groups around the country. Send a SASE to: SHHH, 7910 Woodmont Avenue, Suite 1200, Bethesda, MD 20814. E-mail: national@shhh.org.

The Better Hearing Institute's Helpline gives information on all kinds of hearing problems. Contact American Speech-Language-Hearing Association, 1 Rockville Pike, Rockville, MD 20852, or call 800-638-8255 for information on hearing and help in finding an audiologist (a professional trained to assess hearing loss). The toll-free number is 888-321-ASHA. Web site: www.asha.org.

Beltone Electronics, one of the largest manufacturers of hearing aids, offers free hearing tests at their centers during Better Hearing Month (May). They will also send a free non-operating model of their most popular canal hearing aid to show prospective users how tiny and light a hearing aid can be. Visit their web site to apply for a free sample at www.beltone.com.

The AARP www.aarp.org publishes a report to help older people understand why hearing often declines with age and what products are on the market to help the problem. The report also offers tips on selecting the right equipment. For a free copy send a postcard to Product Report: Hearing Aids (D13766), AARP Fulfillment (EE118), 601 E. St. NW, Washington, DC 20049.

Finally, there is a new telephone service called Dial-A-Hearing Screening Test (DAHST) www.healthy.net. The toll-free national number, 800-222-3277, will direct you to a local number to take the test. When you call the test number, you receive complete instructions for taking the test, which consists of four soft tones for each ear.

Hearing, Speech and Deafness Center (HSDC) www.hsdc.org. Seattle Office: 1620 18th Ave., Seattle, WA 98122-2798. 206-323-5770. Catalog Sales: 206-328-6872 or 1-888-328-2974. HSDC is a nationally unique, fully accredited independent agency offering a broad array of services tailored to help people with a variety of communication problems related to hearing loss and/or speech and language impairments. Approximately 20% of the region's population is hard-of-hearing, speech impaired or deaf. These people face challenges that affect them, their families, friends and colleagues.

HSDC rents assistive communication and signaling devices. Their target rental areas are (1) groups or conferences who need FM equipment, (2) Hotel packages for guest rooms and front desks, and (3) personal alert pagers for post surgical patients who go home from the hospital and need a paging system for only a few weeks. If your business, social gathering or personal requirements dictate the need to rent assistive devices, call the store at 206-328-6872 or E-mail to store@hsdc.org.

You can learn about the causes of hearing loss, receive hearing aid information and the latest research on hearing related disorders from the National Institute on Deafness and Other Communication Disorders. Write them at: NIDCD Clearinghouse, 1 Communication Ave., Bethesda, MD 28092-3456 or call 800-241-1044; or visit them online at: www. nih.gov/nidcd. They will be happy to send you free brochures and answer your questions.

In addition to general problems associated with hearing loss, there are about 6 million people who suffer from tinnitus, a ringing in the ears of bell-like sounds. The symptoms of tinnitus, which occurs more frequently in older persons, cause many people to suffer from sleeplessness, stress, and job-related difficulties. These symptoms are sometimes referred to as Meniere's disease when they include vertigo and dizziness, and can also be associated with hearing loss and fluctuation. For information on tinnitus or a free ropy of a brochure titled "Information About Tinnitus," write to: American Tinnitus Association, PO Box 5, Portland, OR 97207-0005.

Live for Tomorrow—Quit Smoking Today

Many older people dismiss it, but feet and leg pains may be warning signs of more serious disorders and shouldn't be dismissed. They could be symptoms of a circulatory disorder called peripheral arterial disease, or P.A.D. There are many causes of P.A.D.—all either preventable or controllable. They are diabetes, high blood pressure, high cholesterol and smoking. *Smoking is number one.* These can all cause restricted blood flow to the legs because of blockage in the arteries resulting in P.A.D. and possible further complications.

There are so many reasons to quit smoking that I won't list them except to say that you are guaranteed to live longer even if you've been smoking for years. According to the Centers for Disease Control's Office on Smoking and Health, it is worth it to give up smoking at any age. They have lots of information on the health risks associated with smoking and sec-ondhand smoke. Some of their titles include: "Good News for Smokers 50 and Older; It's Never Too Late to Quit," "Out of the Ashes: Choosing a Method to Quit Smoking," and "Don't Let Another Year Go Up In Smoke: Quit Tips."

Look up more information on their web site: www.cdc.gov/tobacco or write them at: 4770 Buford Hwy., NE, Mail Stop K-12, Atlanta, GA 30341. 800-CDC-1311.

For information on P.A.D. write: The Center for Hypertension and Vascular Disease, Wake Forest University Baptist Medical Center, 5th Floor, Janeway Clinical Sciences Building, Medical Center Boulevard, Winston-Salem, North Carolina 27157-1032. 336-716-9623 or The American Diabetes Association, Inc., National Center, 1701 North Beauregard St., Alexandria, VA 22311. Web site: www.wfubmc.edu/hypertension.

Relieving Your Aching Feet and Back

As for our feet and toes, studies show that nearly 90 percent of Americans suffer at one time or another from foot ailments. These can result in headaches, fatigue, grouchiness, and lowered productivity. Some of the more common foot ailments include bunions, heel spurs, corns and calluses, fungus infections, and foot cramps. Check with local podiatry clinics, medical centers, and private podiatry groups to get free or low-cost foot exams and an evaluation of what's ailing your feet.

Back pain affects millions of people and causes millions of dollars in lost wages and productivity from employee absenteeism because of the suffering it causes. Learn more about back care from the American Physical Therapy Association. Write them at: American Physical Therapy Association, PO Box 37257, Washington, DC 20013. They are also on the web at www.atpa.org.

Wear a "Real" Life Saver

In recent years several companies have come out with medical alert tags and identification cards, which contain vital information for police, paramedics, and hospital staffs in case of a medical emergency. Although initially designed with children in mind, they have become very popular with older adults as well.

Medic-Alert is a nonprofit organization whose sole purpose is notify emergency health care professionals about a person's specific conditions. Medic-Alert bracelets and necklaces alert attending persons to conditions such as asthma, heart problems, epilepsy, allergies or diabetes. A lifetime membership includes a steel necklace or bracelet engraved with your personal identification number and a 24 hour telephone number tied into a data bank in California. As a backup you also get an identification card. Personal medical information is updated each year. To join, call 800-432-5378.

Discounts on Drugs

Prescription drugs are one of the most hotly contested issues for seniors today. In many cases, it is nearly impossible to live on a reduced salary or retirement income and be able to afford medicines as today's prices. Even with the government programs and supplemental state programs, the ability for some to pay for their daily medications is prohibitive. However, there are ways to help combat this ongoing problem to make drugs more affordable to mature adults.

To begin with, ask your doctor for as many samples as he will give you. Prescription drug companies are known to give away a lot of samples that doctors can pass on to their patients. This is especially useful when you only need to take the prescriptions for a limited or short length of time.

If you need to fill a prescription, ask your pharmacist for a generic version. This will contain the same ingredients as the name brand, but it many save you up to 50% or more.

Compare prices with drugs, just as you would anything else. Large chain pharmacy departments may offer a lower price than small independent merchants.

Ask your local pharmacy whether they offer senior discounts for medicines and prescription drugs, either through their own club or membership in a senior organization.

Don't overlook the fact that your health insurance or the coverage from you or your spouse's employer may cover a portion of prescription medicines.

Several senior citizen clubs and groups offer their members discounts on prescription medicines. Many of them offer mail-order services as well. In addition, Albertson's (formerly Lucky stores), operating 100 pharmacies in California and Southern Nevada, have a "Lucky 60 Club" whereby anyone 60 or older can receive a 10 percent discount on prescription medications purchased at any Albertson's Pharmacy. Call 1-800-SHOPALB (746-7252).

CVS Pharmacies, with over 800 stores in 14 states covering the Northeast and California, also offer folks over 60 a 10 percent discount on prescriptions. (Customers in New Jersey must be 62 or older.)

The American Association of Retired Persons (AARP) will mail your prescription (as well as thousands of other drugstore products) at a discount and you don't even have to be a member. They have a special department for marketing products for diabetics. Orders are usually shipped within 24 to 48 hours. Call 800-456-2277 for a catalog.

www.drugplace.com offers prescription drugs online. They claim to have very low prices on generic drug orders. Or call 800-881-6325.

Express RX www.expressrx.com. Order prescription drugs through their web site or call them at 501-963-6400.

Merck-Medco Managed Care, LLC www.merck-medco.com. Call your insurance company to see whether they have a contact with this drug company. You may qualify for discounts.

If you are lucky enough to live in one of the ten states that have special drug programs that give big savings for seniors who are not eligible for Medicaid and who don't have private insurance, all you need to do is qualify and you can begin saving immediately. The following programs will send you a form to fill out to qualify:

Connecticut. Conn PACA, PO Box 5011, Hartford, CT 06102. 800-423-5026 (in CT 860-832-9265).

Delaware. Nemours Health Clinic, 915 N. Dupont Blvd., Milford, DE 19963-1092. 302-424-5420; 800-763-9326.

Illinois. Pharmaceutical Assistance Program, Illinois Department of Revenue, PO Box 19021, Springfield, IL 62794; 800624-2459; 217-785-7100.

Maine. Elderly Low-Cost Drug Program. Bureau of Taxation, State Office Building, Agusta, ME 04333-0024. 207-626-8475.

Maryland. Maryland Pharmacy Assistance Program, PO Box 386, Baltimore, MD 21203-0386. 410-767-5397; 800-492-1974.

New Jersey. Pharmaceutical Assistance to the Aged and Disabled (PAAD), Special Benefit Programs, CN 715, Trenton, NJ 08625. 800-792-9745; 609-588-7049.

New York. Elderly Pharmaceutical Insurance Coverage EPIC, PO Box 15018, Albany, NY 12212. 800-332-3742; 518-452-6828.

www.themedicineprogram.com/info.html. This site's function is to assist patients who may qualify to enroll in one or more of the many patient assistance programs now available. These programs provide prescription medicine free of charge to individuals in need, regardless of age if they meet the sponsor's criteria

CHAPTER 7

Associations and Organizations That Work for Mature Adults

There are more people in this country over the age of 55 than there are children in elementary and high school. Mature adults represent a major influence and power that affects nearly every area of American life. In addition to their growing numbers, they control most of this nation's disposable income. As a consequence this group has become a prime target of today's marketplace and a major concern and focus for our lawmakers and politicians.

A large number of national, state, and local organizations, some independent and some linked by vast networks of affiliates, have been created over the past few decades in the United States and Canada. These groups act as advocates and protectors of the rights of those 50 and over. Together, they represent millions of voices demanding action, attention, and respect.

Not only do they provide important information and powerful lobbying services, but many offer special discounts and services for seniors that allow them to enjoy and accomplish many things in life that they would otherwise be unable to afford.

Organizations and associations that operate specifically to serve the needs of mature adults are listed below. By learning about these different groups you can choose which ones most closely match your interests and concerns. There is an enormous amount of information as well as services waiting to be discovered. There are also endless avenues available for working with these groups to improve the quality of life for yourself and other determined, dedicated seniors.

Federal Agencies

Uncle Sam provides us with a wealth of information just for the asking. Below are government agencies that collect and distribute information to the public.

U.S. Department of Commerce
Bureau of the Census Data User Services Division
Washington, DC 20233
800-471-9424

Within the Bureau of the Census is the Census History Staff. As an outgrowth of the collection of data from the census, the "Age Search Program" was begun. This program helps mature adults obtain personal historical information by requesting census records. These census records can help prove age and/or citizenship, and help to obtain a birth certificate, passport, or social security benefits.

> U.S. Department of Health and Human Services
> National Center for Health Services,
> Research and Health
> 8600 Rockville Pike, Building 38A, Room 4S-410,
> Mail Stop 20
> Bethesda, MD 20894
> 301-496-0176
> www.nlm.nih.gov

This agency publishes reports on issues affecting the elderly, especially on the subject of long term care. Request their free publications.

> Social Security Administration
> 6401 Security Blvd.
> Baltimore, MD 21235
> 800-772-1213

Local Social Security offices can help in finding out about senior programs, community groups, and activities in an area. The above toll-free Social Security Administration telephone number operates from 7 A.M. to 7 P.M. throughout the country. Call during off-peak hours, such as 7 to 9 A.M. and 5 to 7 P.M., to receive free information on Social Security Programs, card name changes, earnings statements, Medicare and Medicaid benefits.

U.S. Department of Health and Human Services
National Center for Health Statistics
Hyattsville, MD 20782-2003
301-458-4636
www.cdc.gov

This agency collects data regarding numerous health issues and produces reports for public use. Call them and request to be put on their mailing list. The free reports are published in pamphlets, which most often are summaries on issues of health. Any person on the mailing list is eligible for ordering the in-depth reports, usually 100 pages or more. Request the list of reports that focus particularly on "Health and Aged" and order the ones that interest you.

National Institute on Aging
NIA Information Center
PO Box 8057
Gaithersburg, MD 20898-8057
800-222-2225
www.nih.gov/hia/

The NIA offers many free publications that can be ordered from the Public Information Office. Topics include: accidental hypothermia, aging and alcohol abuse, arthritis advice, cancer facts, exercise, foot care, flu, diabetes, high blood pressure, menopause, hospital hints, using medicines safely, prostrate, long term care, sexuality, smoking and more. They also conduct aging research and publish special reports and clinical summaries on a variety of subjects including health education, health promotion, disease prevention, nutrition, medications and safety.

U.S. Department of Labor
Employment & Training Administration Division
for Older Workers Programs
200 Constitution Ave., NW
Washington, DC 20210
212-535-07713

This is an especially helpful service if you are looking for employment or job training. Currently, the Division of Older Workers offers the following programs:

1. As a result of the Older American Act, the "Part-Time Employment Program" was created for people over age 55. It provides jobs working in community services run by government agencies or nonprofit organizations.

2. Under the Job Training Partnership Act, all ages are eligible for job training services, however, 3 percent of those services (job training) and job placements must be for persons over the age of 55.

Administration on Aging (AOA)
330 Independence Ave., SW
Washington, DC 20201
202-619-0724
www.aoa.dhhs.gov

This umbrella organization functions to oversee all the state Departments on Aging and the Area Agencies on Aging offices around the United States. The focus of these organizations is to provide help to mature adults.

Area Agency on Aging (AAA)

There are more than 700 Area Agencies on Aging that assist mature Americans throughout the United States, assuring such needed services as delivery of hot meals, chore services, energy assistance, adult day care, and transportation assistance. AAA coordinates services for older adults in specific geographic areas. It is an excellent resource for learning about programs for 65+ adults within a specific locale. AAAs are found by checking in the government pages of your telephone directory, or by contacting the State Office of Aging.

Department of Veterans Affairs

www.va.gov

The Department of Veterans Affairs can help veterans and their families with applications for educational assistance, life insurance, home loans and vocational rehabilitation. They also can help with securing medical care and dental benefits. And, as most of us know, they provide burial services to veterans and others who qualify. For information on what benefits and services you are eligible for as a result of serving your country contact: Department of Veteran Affairs, Office of Public Affairs, 810 Vermont Ave., NW, Washington, DC 20420. 800-827-1000.

State Agencies

State Offices on Aging-State Senior Discount Programs. This public organization, also referred to as the "State Unit on Aging," serves as the focal point for all matters relating to the needs of mature persons within a given state. Each state has an Office on Aging as do the District of Columbia and the U.S. territories. You can find your state Office on Aging from one of the following:

- One of the states areas Agencies on Aging.
- The Administration on Aging.
- The National Association of State Units on Aging.
- The Governor's Office.

Or contact the state office listed below. An example of some of the senior services and programs provided include: state senior discounts, senior passport programs, free hunting and fishing licenses, discounts on state park entrance fees and state camping facilities and Long-Term Aging Care, Senior Companion, Brown Bag, Health Care, Adult Day Health Care, and Nutrition.

Alabama. Commission on Aging, State Capitol, Montgomery, AL 36130. 205-261-5743.

Alaska. Older Alaskans Commission, C-Mail Station 0209, Juneau, AK 99811. 907-465-3250.

Arizona. Aging and Adult Administration, 1400 West Washington St., Phoenix, AZ 85007. 602-255-4446.

Arkansas. Office of Aging and Adult Services, Donaghey Building, 7th and Main Streets, Little Rock, AR 72201. 501-371-2441.

California. Department of Aging, 1020 19th Street, Sacramento, CA 95814. 916-322-5290.

Colorado. Aging and Adult Service Division, Department of Social Services, 717 17th Street, Denver, CO 80218. 303-294-5913.

Connecticut. Department of Aging, 175 Main Street Hartford, CT 06106. 203- 566-3238.

Delaware. Division on Aging, Department of Health and Social Services, 1901 North Dupont Highway, New Castle, DE 19720. 302-421-6791.

District Of Columbia. Office of Aging, 1424 K Street NW, Washington, DC 20011. 202-724-5626.

Florida. Program Office of Aging and Adult Services, 1317 Winewood Blvd., Tallahassee, FL 32301. 904-488-8922.

Georgia. Office of Aging, 878 Peachtree Street, NE, Atlanta, GA 30309. 404-894-5333.

Hawaii. Executive Office on Aging, Office of the Governor, 335 Merchant Street, Honolulu, HI 96813. 808-548-2593.

Idaho. Office on Aging, Statehouse Room 114, Boise, ID 83720. 208-334-3833.

Illinois. Department on Aging, 421 East Capitol Avenue, Springfield, IL 62701. 217-785-2870.

Indiana. Department on Aging and Community Services, 251 North Illinois Street, Indianapolis, IN 46207. 317-232-7006.

Iowa. Department of Elder Affairs, 914 Grand Avenue, Des Moines, IA 50319. 515-281-5187.

Kansas. Department on Aging, 610 West Tenth, Topeka, KS 66612. 913-296-4986.

Kentucky. Division for Aging Services, Department of Human Resources, 275 East Main Street, Frankfort, KY 40601. 502-564-6930.

Louisiana. Office of Elderly Affairs, PO Box 80374, Baton Rouge, LA 70898. 504-925-1700.

Maine. Bureau of Maine's Elderly State House, Station No. 11, Augusta, ME 04333. 207-289-2561.

Maryland. Office on Aging, 301 W. Preston St., Baltimore, MD 21201. 301-225-1100.

Massachusetts. Department of Elder Affairs, 38 Chauncey St., Boston, MA 02111. 617-727-7750.

Michigan. Office of Services to the Aging, P.O. Box 30026, Lansing, MI 48909. 517-373-8230.

Minnesota. Board on Aging, 204 Metro Square Building, 7th and Roberts Streets, St. Paul, MN 55101. 612-296-2544.

Mississippi. Council on Aging, 301 West Pearl St., Jackson, MS 39203. 601-949-2070.

Missouri. Division on Aging, Department of Social Services, 505 Missouri Blvd., Jefferson City, MO 65102. 314-751-3082.

Montana. Community Services Division, PO Box 4210, Helena, MT 59604. 406-444-3865.

Nebraska. Department on Aging. 301 Centennial Mall, South Lincoln, NE 68509. 402-471-2306.

Nevada. Division on Aging, Department of Human Resources, 505 East King Street, Carson City, NV 89710. 702-885-4210.

New Hampshire. Council on Aging, 105 London Road, Building No. 3, 9th Floor, Concord, NH 03301. 603-271-2751.

Ohio. Department of Aging, 50 West Broad Street, Columbus, OH 42315. 614-466-5500.

New Jersey. Division on Aging, Department of Community Affairs, 363 West State Street, Trenton, NJ 08625. 609-292-4833.

New Mexico. State Agency On Aging, 224 East Palace Avenue, Santa Fe, NM 87501. 505-827-7640.

New York. Office for the Aging, New York State Plaza, Agency Building No. 2, Albany, NY 12223. 518-474-4425.

North Carolina. Division on Aging, 1985 Umpstead Drive, Raleigh, NC 27603. 919-733-3983.

North Dakota. Aging Services, Department of Human Services, State Capitol, Bismarck, ND 58505. 701-224-2577.

Ohio. Department on Aging, 50 West Broad Street, 9th Floor, Columbus, OH 42315. 614-466-5500.

Oklahoma. Special Unit on Aging, Department of Human Services, P.O. Box 25352, Oklahoma City, OK 73125. 405-521-2281.

Oregon. Senior Services Division, 313 Public Service Building, Salem, OR 97310. 503-378-4728.

Pennsylvania. Department of Aging, 231 State Street, Harrisburg, PA 17101. 717-783-1550.

Puerto Rico. Gericulture Commission, Department of Social Services, P.O. Box 11398, Santurce, PR 00910. 809-721-4010.

South Carolina. Commission on Aging, 915 Main Street, Columbia, SC 29201. 803-758-2576.

South Dakota. Office of Adult Services and Aging, 700 North Illinois Street, Pierre, SD 57501. 605-773-3656.

Tennessee. Commission on Aging, 535 Church Street, Nashville, TN 37219. 615-741-2056.

Texas. Department on Aging, 1949 IH-35 South. P.O. Box 12786, Capitol Station, Austin, TX 78741. 512-444-2727.

Utah. Division of Aging and Adult Services, Department of Social Services, 150 West North Temple, Salt Lake City, UT 84145. 801-533-6422.

Vermont. Office on Aging, 103 South Main Street, Waterbury, VT 05676. 802-241-2400.

Virgin Islands. Commission on Aging, 6F Havensight Mall, Charlotte Amalie St. Thomas, VI 00801. 809-774-5884.

Virginia. Department on Aging, 18th Floor, 101 North 14th Street, Richmond, VA 23219. 804-225-2271.

Washington. Aging and Adult Services, Department of Social and Health Services, OB-43G Olympia, WA 98504. 206-753-2502.

West Virginia. Commission on Aging, Holly Grove, State Capitol, Charleston, WV 25305. 304-348-3317.

Wisconsin. Bureau of Aging, Division of Community Services, One West Wilson Street, Madison, WI 53702. 608-266-2536.

Wyoming. Commission on Aging, Hathaway Building—Room 139, Cheyenne, WY 82002. 307-777-7986.

More Public Agencies

Catholic Charities Foster Grandparent Program
2625 Zanker Road, Suite 200
San Jose, California 95134-2107
408-944-0668
www.ccsj.org

Coastline Elderly Services Foster Grandparent Program
1646 Purchase Street
New Bedford, MA 02740
508-999-6400
www.coastlineelderly.org
E-mail: information@coastlineelderly.org

National Senior Service Corps (formerly ACTION)
1201 New York Ave., NW
Washington, DC 20525
800-424-8867
www.seniorcorps.org or www.nationalservice.org
The National Senior Service Corps is a national network of projects that place older volunteers in volunteer assignments in their communities. There

are three umbrella programs. One is the Foster Grandparent Program, which links senior volunteers to children who need their help. Another is the Senior Companion Program, which places its volunteers with adults needing extra assistance. The third, the Retired and Senior Volunteer Program (RSVP) is "One stop shopping" for senior volunteers. Senior Corps Programs operate in local communities throughout the U.S. For a complete list of Foster Grandparent Agency Programs, call 202-606-5000.

U.S. Department of Health and Human Services
Health Care Financing Administration (HCFA)
202-619-0257
www.hhs.gov
HFMA is responsible for funding and administering the Medicare program. It also assists in the fulfilling of this responsibility for the various Medicaid programs. The agency is an excellent resource for information about health care expenses, use of medical services and insurance coverage for those 65 and older.

Service Corps of Retired Executives (SCORE)
Small Business Administration
1129 20th St., NW
Washington, DC 20036
800-634-0245
www.score.org
SCORE utilizes retired and semi-retired businessmen to counsel new and existing small businesses. Volunteers are usually retired business professionals who want to share their expertise, experience and

knowledge with the up and coming generation of business owners. Over 13,000 SCORE members volunteer nationwide. If you are interested in this program contact: SCORE, 409 Third St., SW, Fourth Floor, Washington DC 20024. 202-205-6762; 800-634-0245.

U.S. House Select Committee on Aging
G31 Dirksen Senate Building
Washington, DC 20510-6400
202-224-5364
www.senate.gov/~aging

U.S. Senate Special Committee on Aging
United States Senate, SD-G31
Washington, DC 20510
202-224-5364
www.senate.gov/-aging

Both the House Select Committee on aging and its counterpart in the Senate are great places to find out about existing, pending or anticipated legislation involving older adults. Send for free copies of special reports on a variety of topics from prescription drug price increases to women's health issues.

Private Organizations

American Association of Retired Persons (AARP)
Office of Communications
601 E St, NW Washington, DC 20049
800-424-3410.
www.aarp.com

AARP, the American Association of Retired Persons, is a nonprofit, nonpartisan organization dedicated to helping older Americans achieve lives of independence, dignity and purpose.

Founded in 1958, AARP is the nation's oldest and largest organization of older Americans, with a membership of more than 35 million. Membership is open to anyone age 50 or older, whether working or retired. AARP's motto is to "serve, not to be served." Membership dues (including spouse) are $8 for one year. AARP members receive *Modern Maturity* magazine bi-monthly, and *AARP News Bulletin* 11 times per year. *Modern Maturity* has the second largest circulation of any U.S. magazine. The Association also distributes a wide range of specialized publications, many of which are available free of charge.

The Retired Teachers Division is open to former members of the National Retired Teachers Association and to soon-to-retire teachers, administrators, and other education professionals. Members receive the NRTA News Bulletin and the NRTA edition of *Modern Maturity* magazine.

AARP Priorities include four major areas that affect the quality of life that the AARP has targeted for a significant portion of its resources. These issue "initiatives" include: Health Care Campaign, Women's Initiative, Worker Equity, and Minority Affairs Initiative. AARP represents a diverse population that includes workers and retirees, women re-entering the workforce, frail women over 80 living alone, people with comfortable standards of living, and those who struggle daily. A major AARP commitment is the development of legislative policy recommendations serving such a diverse group of older Americans.

AARP Member Services:

- Purchase Privilege Program. Provides members with discounts at major car rental companies, motel and hotel chains, recreational and tourist facilities.
- Pharmacy Service. Provides prescription medicines and other health care items to members by mail or direct purchase.
- Travel Service. A wide variety of escorted or independent travel opportunities, i.e., tours, cruises, special-event programs and hosted living abroad programs, designed for AARP mature travelers.
- AARP Motoring Service. Includes a customized plan provided by AMOCO Motor Club. Members of the AARP Motoring Plan receive 20 road service benefits.
- Group Health Insurance. Underwritten for AARP members by the Prudential Insurance Company.
- Auto/Homeowners Insurance. Offered by The Hartford Insurance Group to Association members.
- Mobile Home Insurance. Insurance for mobile home owners is provided by the Foremost Insurance Group.
- Educational Resources. AARP produces audiovisual program kits on issues ranging from health and nutrition, housing, and retirement planning to consumer protection and crime prevention. The kits are loaned free of charge to nonprofit organizations providing services to older people and members of the aging network.

The organization also publishes a continuing series of books of special usefulness and importance to middle-aged and older readers. Subjects include: money management, retirement planning, insurance decisions, foot care, crime prevention, widowhood, funeral planning, and housing alternatives.

AARP publications include more than 140 titles available free of charge upon request. These authoritative materials cover a variety of topics including health, consumer affairs, crime prevention, retirement planning, lifetime learning, and driver re-education. Information ranges from practical advice to "how-to" guides, demographics to resource publications. For a complete list of publications write: AARP Fulfillments, EE0073, 601 E St. NW, Washington, DC 20049.

Community Services. More than 400,000 AARP volunteers are involved in community service programs nationwide that reinforce self-worth and self-reliance among older people. Through these programs, older Americans are given the opportunity to share their wisdom, experience, and abilities with those of all ages in need.

Some other beneficial programs administered by the AARP and its more than 3,700 local chapters and 2,500 Retired Teacher Association units throughout the United States include: Consumer Affairs Program, Criminal Justice Service, 55 Alive/Mature Driving, Health Advocacy Services, Housing Program, Institute of Lifetime Learning, Intergenerational Program, International Activities, Inter-religious Liaison, Legal Counsel for the Elderly, National Gerontology Resource Center, National Retired Teachers Association Activities,

Senior Community Service Employment Program, Tax Aide Program, and Widowed Persons Service.

For a complete description of their services look up the web site at www.aarp.com.

Sears Mature Outlook
6001 N. Clark St.
Chicago, IL 60660-9977
800-265-3675

Sponsored by Sears, the country's largest retailer, this club specializes in discounts, some of them substantial, on products and services in its stores, plus many other benefits for folks over 50. The annual fee is $19.99, which includes your spouse. Some of their services and benefits include:

- *Mature Outlook* magazine, a readable, artfully designed magazine with articles and columns full of practical information aimed towards mature adults.
- *Mature Outlook Newsletter*, also a source of useful facts and tips.
- $320 in "Sears Money" that can be used like cash on any merchandise or Sears services. These certificates are unrestricted and can be used for purchases in any store or Sears catalog. "Bonus Club" merchandise certificates from Sears are issued for accumulated purchases to customers using Sears Charge accounts.
- Automotive service, a coupon book redeemable at Sears Automotive Centers for discounts on various maintenance jobs.

- "Travel Alert" with savings up to 50 percent for domestic and international tours, cruises, and last-minute bookings at even bigger savings. Join now and receive 1,500 Sears bonus points. 888-884-4359.
- Discounts of 10 to 20 percent off the room rates and 10 percent off meals at participating Holiday Inns and Crowne Plaza Hotels. Also discounts on car rentals from Budget/Sears, Hertz, Avis, and National.
- Mail-order pharmacy discounts.
- 10 percent off the membership charge for the Allstate Motor Club.
- 20 percent discount on eyewear products at participating Sears Optical Departments. Plus "Vision One" membership for up to 50 percent on glasses, contacts, fashion frames, and eye care services.
- Savings on service fees on Citicorp Traveler's Checks.
- $5,000 Travel Accident Insurance for members and $5,000 for their spouse.

Senior Citizens Law Center
3435 Wilshire Blvd, Suite 2869
Los Angeles, CA 90010
213-639-0930
This is a legal services support center specializing in the legal problems of the elderly. It acts as an advocate on behalf of elderly and poor clients in legislative

and administrative affairs. Contact them for copies of handbooks, testimonies and guides.

In Washington: 1101 14th NW, Suite 400, Washington, DC 20005. 202-289-6976.

American Society on Aging
833 Market Street, Suite 511
San Francisco, CA 94103. 415-974-9600.
www.asaging.org.
E-mail: info@asaging.org

Members include senior citizens, students, business persons, educators, researchers, administrators, health care and social service professionals who work to enhance the well being of older individuals and create unity among those working with and for the elderly. It focuses on the interests and needs of older people worldwide, particularly in the Third World. Besides offering continuing education programs on age-related issues, the American Society on Aging generates two important publications: Generations, a journal that provides practical current information in the field of aging, with emphasis on medical and social practice, research, and policy; and The Aging Connection, a bimonthly newspaper that covers critical events and issues in the field of aging.

National Interfaith Coalition on Aging
E-mail: info@ncoa.org
409 Third Street SW
Washington, DC 20024
202-479-1200
www.ncoa.org/nica/nica.html

This group promotes and provides resources for ministries with older Adults. NICA works with more than 25 Protestant, Jewish, Catholic, and orthodox organizations to provide training and develop resources through local congregations and religious organizations. They approach senior issues by representing the spiritual concerns of older Americans in public and private forums. Membership is $45 annually.

Catholic Golden Age
RD #2, Box 161
Olyphant, PA 18477
800-836-5699
www.catholicgoldenage.org
A nonprofit association of senior citizens founded in 1975, Catholic Golden Age provides spiritual benefits as well as material benefits and discounts to men and women age 50 and over. Currently Catholic golden Age has over 400,000 members.

For updated discounts check the web site: www.catholicgoldenage.org

Jewish Association for Services for the Aged
132 West 31st St.
New York, NY 10001
212-273-5200
www.interport.net/jasa/index.html
Established on the East Coast in 1968, this social welfare organization provides the services necessary to enable older adults to remain in the community. There are over 60,000 members, served in New York

City and Nassau and Suffolk counties. Services include: information and referral to appropriate health, welfare, educational, social, recreational, and vacation services, government benefits and entitlements; personal counseling; financial assistance; health and medical service counseling; counseling on housing and long-term care; homemaker service; group educational and recreational activities; hot lunch programs; referral to summer camps; legal services; protective services; reaching out to the isolated; and programs for the independent senior clubs.

> National Council on Aging
> 409 Third St. SW
> Washington DC 20024
> 202-479-1200
> www.ncoa.org
> E-mail: info@ncoa.org

NCOA is the nation's first association of organizations dedicated to promoting the dignity, self-determination, well being and contributions of older persons. Members help community organizations to enhance the lives of older adults, turn creative ideas into programs and services that help older people in hundreds of communities, and assume a national voice as a powerful advocate for public policies, societal attitudes, and business practices that promote vital aging. Offices located in Cincinnati, OH, Ft. Lauderdale, FL, Hempstead, NY, Los Angeles, CA, Bangor, ME, Trenton, NJ, New York City, NY, San Francisco, CA, San Jose, CA and West Palm Beach, FL.

National Association of Retired Federal
Employees (NAFRE)
1533 New Hampshire Ave., NW
Washington, DC 20036
202-234-0832
www.narfe.org

This is an association of federal retirees and their
families. They represent an aggressive lobbying force
on Capitol Hill whose purpose is to protect retirement
benefits. Membership includes an annual subscription to *Retirement Life* magazine, and membership in
a local chapter. Other NAFRE benefits include:

- Discounts on Avis and Hertz car rentals.
- Travel discounts.
- Up to 50 percent savings on worldwide cruises.
- NARFE VISA with no annual fee for six months.
- Vision care program with free sight evaluations
  and discounts on eyewear.
- United Airlines' Silver Wings Plus Travel Club
  membership for those over 60, plus tours, hotel,
  car-rental savings, and airline discounts; long-
  term care insurance plan.

Older Women's League (OWL)
332 S. Michigan Avenue, Suite 1050
Chicago, Illinois 60604
312-347-0011 or 800-TAKE-OWL.
www.members.aol.com/owl/il

In this country, the problems of aging are largely
women's problems. More than 70 percent of the nearly
4 million persons over 65 living in poverty are women.
Fewer than 20 percent of older women currently receive

any pension income. Most women over 65 depend on Social Security as their only significant income. Millions of mid-life women have no health insurance.

The Older Women's League works to change these facts. It is the first grassroots membership organization to focus exclusively on women as they age. OWL works to provide mutual support for its members, helps them achieve economic and social equity, and works to improve the image and status of older women. It provides educational materials, training for citizen advocates, and informational publications dealing with the important issues facing women as they grow older. Members are eligible for supplemental insurance plans, receive the OWL Observer newspaper, and receive discounts on all OWL publications. Washington location: 661 11th St. NW, Washington, DC 20001. 202-783-6686.

American Legion
P.O. Box 1055
Indianapolis, IN 46206
www.legion.org

The American Legion is the nation's largest veterans organization. While it isn't made up solely of those 50+, it does include a large group of older veterans. *American Legion Magazine*, for example, has a circulation of more than 2.5 million. Its average reader is 60 years old. The Legion's most visible activity is its work on behalf of veterans, their survivors, and dependents. In addition, a large portion of the American Legion's resources are channeled into education programs and citizenship activities for youths. Each year more than

200 American Legion community service projects costing more than $5 million in aid touch the lives of millions of Americans.

Note: Service organizations such as the Rotary, Lions, Kiwanis, and Elks also have large age 50+ constituencies. These groups also have both local and regional clubs.

National Caucus and Center on the Black Aged
1424 K St., NW, Suite 500
Washington, DC 20005
202-637-8400
www.ncba-blackaged.org

This organization seeks to improve living conditions for low-income elderly Black Americans. They advocate changes in federal and state laws by improving the economic, health, and social status of low-income senior citizens. They also promote community awareness of problems and issues affecting this group. It operates an employment program involving older persons in 14 states and sponsors, owns, and manages rental housing for the elderly.

National Hispanic Council on Aging
2713 Ontario Road, NW
Washington, DC 20009
202-265-1288

Members of this organization work for the well-being of the Hispanic elderly through research, policy analysis, and projects, and provide a network for organizations and community groups interested in the Hispanic elderly.

National Association of Hispanic Elderly
The Association Nacional Pro Personas Mayores
1452 West Temple St, Suite 100
Los Angeles, CA 90026-1724
213 487-1922.

This organization focuses on helping rural elderly in southern Texas and northern California to gain access to supportive services offered under the Older Americans Act. Trained volunteers help the elderly obtain needed assistance and local services.

National Indian Council on Aging
PO 10501 Montgomery Blvd N.E., Suite 210
Albuquerque NM 87111
505-292-2001
www.nicoa.org

This organization seeks to bring about improved, comprehensive services to the Indian and Alaskan native elderly. It acts as a focal point for the articulation of the needs of the Indian elderly, disseminates information on Indian aging programs, provides technical assistance and training opportunities to tribal organizations, and conducts research on the needs of Indian elderly.

National Pacific/Asian Resource Center
1511 3rd Avenue, Suite 914
Seattle, WA 98101-1626
206-624-1221 or 800-336-2722

This group's goals are to ensure and improve the delivery of health and social services to elderly Pacific/Asians and increase the capabilities of community-based services to the elderly. They also produce several informative publications and a national community service directory. $10 yearly fee.

National Committee to Preserve Social Security and Medicare (NCPSSM)
2000 K St., NW, Suite 800
Washington, DC 20006
202-822-9459
www.ncpssm.org

The NCPSSM is a highly vocal organization and one of the largest lobbying groups in America dealing with Social Security, Medicare, and other senior issues on Capitol Hill.

National Alliance of Senior Citizens (NASC)
525 Wilson Blvd.
Arlington, VA 22201
703-528-4380

This national lobbying organization is targeted to a politically conservative audience. There are more than 2 million members working to promote the advancement of senior Americans through sound fiscal policy. Their purpose is to inform the American public of the needs of senior citizens and of the programs and policies being carried out by the government and other groups. Members' benefits include life insurance plan; VISA card with no fee for six months; newsletters; and discounts on lodging, car rentals, moving expenses, and a motoring club. Dues are $10 a year ($15 for a couple).

The Retired Officers Association
201 N. Washington St.
Alexandria, VA 22314-2529
800-245-TROA

This association is an independent nonprofit organization dedicated to maintaining a strong national defense and preserving the entitlements and benefits of uniformed services personnel, their families, and survivors. TROA is the largest military officers' association in the country. Members receive *The Retired Officers Magazine*, containing reports on Congress and matters of special interest. Other benefits include counseling in employment assistance, personal affairs, dependent scholarship loans/grants, survivor assistance, and retirement information. There are also discounts on car rentals, a discount travel program, health screenings, sports holidays, a mail-order prescription program, group health and life insurance plans, financial services, and an extended car warranty program. Yearly membership is $50. Lifetime membership ranges from $275–$360 depending on your age.

Spry Foundation
10 G Street, N.E., Suite 600,
Washington, DC 20002
202-216-0401.
www.spry.org.
E-mail: spryfoundation@ncpssm.org

SPRY helps older adults plan for a healthy and financially secure future.

Canadian Association of Retired Persons (C.A.R.P.)
27 Queen Street East, Suite 304
Toronto, Ontario M5C 2M6 Canada
800-363-9736
www.fifty-plus.net
This organization is a national nonprofit, nonpolitical association of Canadians over 50 established to promote the interests of mature Canadians. Membership is $16 a year (including spouse). This group is the Canadian counterpart to the AARP, and has over 375,000 members. Benefits include "C.A.R.P. News" newsletter, discounts on health care, home and car insurance, car rentals, hotels, theaters, and travel.

Did You Know?

- 75% of seniors on the net have a college degree
- 39% have a graduate degree
- 45% have household incomes of $75,000 or more
- 26% have incomes of $100,000 or more
- More than 50% have investments worth more than $100,000

Knowledgeable seniors are empowered seniors!

More Free Gifts and Incredible Bargains!

Do you own a dog, cat, bird, horse, fish, reptile, or other type of pet? Then you're going to love **Free Stuff & Good Deals for Your Pet**. It features goods and services that are either absolutely free or are such a fantastic deal, you won't want to pass them up! And best of all, author and professional bargain hunter Linda Bowman shows you how to obtain your free gifts and incredible bargains quickly and easily. This fact-filled guide is packed with information on where to find:

- Free Pet Adoptions
- Free Food for Your Pet
- Free and Low Cost Health Care
- Pet Insurance Bargains
- Pet Grooming Discounts
- Free Toys and Treats
- Free Obedience Training
- Free Magazines, Newsletters, Catalogs and Books
- Free Pet Shows and Contests
- Incredible Shopping Bargains
- Pet Organizations and Associations
. . . and much more!

$12.95
1-800-784-9553

More Free Gifts and Incredible Bargains!

Have you discovered the joy of surfing the World Wide Web? Then you're going to love **Free Stuff & Good Deals on the Internet**. It features goods and services that are either absolutely free or are such a fantastic deal, you won't want to pass them up! And best of all, author and professional bargain hunter Linda Bowman shows you how to obtain your free gifts and incredible bargains quickly and easily. This fact-filled guide is packed with information on where to find:

- Free Money on the Internet
- Free Expert Advice
- Incredible Travel Bargains
- Free Health Care Information
- Free Financial and Legal Advice
- Free Educational Opportunities
- Free Business Opportunities
- Incredible Shopping Bargains
- Free Magazines, Newsletters, Catalogs and Books
- Free Stuff for Kids and Their Parents
- Organizations and Associations
. . . and much more!

$12.95
1-800-784-9553

BOOK DESCRIPTIONS

The Book of Good Habits
Simple and Creative Ways to Enrich Your Life
by Dirk Mathison
224 pages $9.95

Café Nation
Coffee Folklore, Magick, and Divination
by Sandra Mizumoto Posey
224 pages $9.95

Collecting Sins
A Novel
by Steven Sobel
288 pages $13

FREE Stuff & Good Deals for Folks over 50
by Linda Bowman
240 pages $12.95

FREE Stuff & Good Deals for Your Pet
by Linda Bowman
240 pages $12.95

FREE Stuff & Good Deals on the Internet
by Linda Bowman
240 pages $12.95

Health Care Handbook
A Consumer's Guide to the American Health Care System
by Mark Cromer
256 pages $12.95

Helpful Household Hints
The Ultimate Guide to Housekeeping
by June King
224 pages $12.95

How To Find Your Family Roots and Write Your Family History
by William Latham and Cindy Higgins
288 pages $14.95

How To Win Lotteries, Sweepstakes, and Contests in the 21st Century
by Steve "America's Sweepstakes King" Ledoux
224 pages $14.95

Letter Writing Made Easy!
Featuring Sample Letters for Hundreds of Common Occasions
by Margaret McCarthy
224 pages $12.95

Letter Writing Made Easy! Volume 2
Featuring More Sample Letters for Hundreds of Common Occasions
by Margaret McCarthy
224 pages $12.95

Nancy Shavick's Tarot Universe
by Nancy Shavick
336 pages $15.95

Offbeat Food
Adventures in an Omnivorous World
by Alan Ridenour
240 pages $19.95

Offbeat Golf
A Swingin' Guide To a Worldwide Obsession
by Bob Loeffelbein
192 pages $17.95

Offbeat Marijuana
The Life and Times of the World's Grooviest Plant
by Saul Rubin
240 pages $19.95

Offbeat Museums
The Collections and Curators of America's Most Unusual Museums
by Saul Rubin
240 pages $19.95

Past Imperfect
How Tracing Your Family Medical History Can Save Your Life
by Carol Daus
240 pages $12.95

Quack!
Tales of Medical Fraud from the Museum of Questionable Medical Devices
by Bob McCoy
240 pages $19.95

The Seven Sacred Rites of Menopause
The Spiritual Journey to the Wise-Woman Years
by Kristi Meisenbach Boylan
144 pages $11.95

Silent Echoes
Discovering Early Hollywood Through the Films of Buster Keaton
by John Bengtson
240 pages $24.95

What's Buggin' You?
Michael Bohdan's Guide to Home Pest Control
by Michael Bohdan
256 pages $12.95

BOOK DESCRIPTIONS

The Book of Good Habits
Simple and Creative Ways to Enrich Your Life
by Dirk Mathison
224 pages $9.95

Café Nation
Coffee Folklore, Magick, and Divination
by Sandra Mizumoto Posey
224 pages $9.95

Collecting Sins
A Novel
by Steven Sobel
288 pages $13

FREE Stuff & Good Deals for Folks over 50
by Linda Bowman
240 pages $12.95

FREE Stuff & Good Deals for Your Pet
by Linda Bowman
240 pages $12.95

FREE Stuff & Good Deals on the Internet
by Linda Bowman
240 pages $12.95

Health Care Handbook
A Consumer's Guide to the American Health Care System
by Mark Cromer
256 pages $12.95

Helpful Household Hints
The Ultimate Guide to Housekeeping
by June King
224 pages $12.95

How To Find Your Family Roots and Write Your Family History
by William Latham and Cindy Higgins
288 pages $14.95

How To Win Lotteries, Sweepstakes, and Contests in the 21st Century
by Steve "America's Sweepstakes King" Ledoux
224 pages $14.95

Letter Writing Made Easy!
Featuring Sample Letters for Hundreds of Common Occasions
by Margaret McCarthy
224 pages $12.95

Letter Writing Made Easy! Volume 2
Featuring More Sample Letters for Hundreds of Common Occasions
by Margaret McCarthy
224 pages $12.95

Nancy Shavick's Tarot Universe
by Nancy Shavick
336 pages $15.95

Offbeat Food
Adventures in an Omnivorous World
by Alan Ridenour
240 pages $19.95

Offbeat Golf
A Swingin' Guide To a Worldwide Obsession
by Bob Loeffelbein
192 pages $17.95

Offbeat Marijuana
The Life and Times of the World's Grooviest Plant
by Saul Rubin
240 pages $19.95

Offbeat Museums
The Collections and Curators of America's Most Unusual Museums
by Saul Rubin
240 pages $19.95

Past Imperfect
How Tracing Your Family Medical History Can Save Your Life
by Carol Daus
240 pages $12.95

Quack!
Tales of Medical Fraud from the Museum of Questionable Medical Devices
by Bob McCoy
240 pages $19.95

The Seven Sacred Rites of Menopause
The Spiritual Journey to the Wise-Woman Years
by Kristi Meisenbach Boylan
144 pages $11.95

Silent Echoes
Discovering Early Hollywood Through the Films of Buster Keaton
by John Bengtson
240 pages $24.95

What's Buggin' You?
Michael Bohdan's Guide to Home Pest Control
by Michael Bohdan
256 pages $12.95

ORDER FORM
1-800-784-9553

	Quantity	Amount
The Book of Good Habits ($9.95)	_____	_____
Café Nation ($9.95)	_____	_____
Collecting Sins ($13)	_____	_____
FREE Stuff & Good Deals for Folks over 50 ($12.95)	_____	_____
FREE Stuff & Good Deals for Your Pet ($12.95)	_____	_____
FREE Stuff & Good Deals on the Internet ($12.95)	_____	_____
Health Care Handbook ($12.95)	_____	_____
Helpful Household Hints ($12.95)	_____	_____
How to Find Your Family Roots . . . ($14.95)	_____	_____
How to Win Lotteries, Sweepstakes, and Contests . . . ($14.95)	_____	_____
Letter Writing Made Easy! ($12.95)	_____	_____
Letter Writing Made Easy! Volume 2 ($12.95)	_____	_____
Nancy Shavick's Tarot Universe ($15.95)	_____	_____
Offbeat Food ($19.95)	_____	_____
Offbeat Golf ($17.95)	_____	_____
Offbeat Marijuana ($19.95)	_____	_____
Offbeat Museums ($19.95)	_____	_____
Past Imperfect ($12.95)	_____	_____
Quack! ($19.95)	_____	_____
The Seven Sacred Rites of Menopause ($11.95)	_____	_____
Silent Echoes ($24.95)	_____	_____
What's Buggin' You? ($12.95)	_____	_____

	Subtotal	_____
Shipping & Handling:	CA residents add 8% sales tax	_____
1 book — $3.00	Shipping and Handling (see left)	_____
Each additional book is $ .50	**TOTAL**	_____

Name _____

Address _____

City _____ State _____ Zip _____

☐ Visa ☐ MasterCard Card No.: _____

Exp. Date _____ Signature _____

☐ Enclosed is my check or money order payable to:

Santa Monica Press LLC
P.O. Box 1076
Santa Monica, CA 90406
www.santamonicapress.com

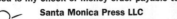

1-800-784-9553